THE READING CONNECTION

THE READING CONNECTION
Bringing Parents, Teachers, and Librarians Together

Elizabeth Knowles

and

Martha Smith

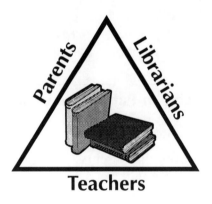

1997
LIBRARIES UNLIMITED, INC.
Englewood, Colorado

LIBRARIES UNLIMITED, INC.
P.O. Box 6633
Englewood, CO 80155-6633
1-800-237-6124

Production Editor: Kay Mariea
Copy Editor: Brooke D. Graves
Proofreader: Lori D. Kranz
Design and Layout: Pamela J. Getchell

Library of Congress Cataloging-in-Publication Data

Knowles, Elizabeth, 1946-
    The reading connection : bringing parents, teachers, and
librarians together / Elizabeth Knowles and Martha Smith.
    x, 117p. 22x28 cm.
    Includes bibliographical references.
    ISBN 1-56308-436-8
    1. Reading--Parent participation.   2. Book clubs.   3. Children--
Books and reading.   I. Smith, Martha, 1946-   . II. Title.
LB1050.2.K66   1997
372.41--dc20   96-42451
                                                                  CIP

CONTENTS

INTRODUCTION

The purpose of this book is to provide teachers, librarians, and parents with information for establishing a book club for the school community. Book club members explore current children's literature and help children become lifelong readers. Efforts to encourage children to read are essential in light of current trends which indicate that children are reading less and less each year. Developing lifelong readers can be achieved most easily through a home and school partnership. The topics and sample book club sessions contained in this book involve literature for prekindergarten through eighth-grade students.

BOOK CLUB BEGINNINGS

The idea for a book club for parents in our school began with a parent's very real distress over what her daughter was reading from our school library. Being an affluent private school with strict entrance requirements meant we had many excellent young readers. These students tend to read by author, and some of our third graders can easily handle young adult reading—but the topics and sophistication of some of these books upset this parent.

Therefore, we developed our book club to inform parents about what is available and popular in children's literature today and to encourage parents to be knowledgeable about and involved in their children's reading choices. The bibliographies and handouts we made available to the parents were key to our success.

In the more than four years we have organized a book club, we feel we have met and exceeded our original expectations. Our club has been for parents, and we usually had about 30 parents attend meetings. The group is fluid; interested parents who learn of the group in the middle of the year are welcome to join.

Parents joined our club to learn more about children's literature. We have found that, after attending club meetings, participants tend to read more often and longer with their children, and their children tend to read more on their own. These parents also come to us for reading suggestions and to share information and ideas.

It has been our experience that a book club helps alleviate and answer parents' concerns about the content of children's literature today. We strongly recommend, however, that the moderators and sponsors of a book club be knowledgeable about the school's or district's policies for handling concerns. This point is discussed further in chapter 1.

While we established our book club initially for parents, the programs suggested in this book could easily be modified for a book club for teachers or students. A combination of parents with children or teachers with students may also be good options in some schools. If the moderators have the time, they could set up one club for parents and another club for students. All combinations are possible, and this book could be applied to all situations. Our goal is to steer librarians, teachers, parents, and students toward good and appropriate selections, while encouraging and nurturing a love for reading.

CHILDREN AND BOOKS

Choosing the best books for children is a difficult task. New titles, authors, and series are continuously available in bookstores. Children who read well come from homes where there are many books, magazines, and newspapers. Their parents make time for reading and place importance and value on reading aloud to their children from an early age.

Not all of our participants had children who loved to read, so this book club was especially important to them. We also had parents who knew the importance of reading aloud to their preschool children but needed encouragement and guidance in making selections for school-age children. We helped all parents become familiar with specific books and authors and suggested ways to encourage reading. Through discussion, members of the group also shared ideas with each other concerning ways to stimulate reading in the home.

Parents have the responsibility to talk to their children, ask questions that require reflection, stimulate curiosity, and encourage their children to talk about travels and experiences. All too often children spend free time watching television or videos and playing video games instead of reading. Parents need to turn the television and video games off and turn their children on to reading. The best way to do this is to read to them, starting at an early age with picture books and continuing through the middle school years.

The Association of Booksellers for Children uses the slogan, "The most important twenty minutes of your day!" to encourage reading aloud to children. The Association feels that reading is so important that pediatricians should recommend reading to children as part of a daily routine like dental hygiene, good nutrition, and the standard inoculations. Reading aloud should be part of every school day, and every child should have books at home.

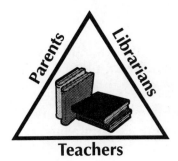

Chapter 1

Starting a Book Club

INTRODUCTION

A book club brings together members of the school community to discuss and learn about children's literature and to encourage children to read. Depending on the makeup of the particular school community, the club moderators may choose to include parents, children, teachers, librarians, or a combination of these groups among club participants. In each case, the goal is to foster knowledge about children's books and an enthusiastic joy of reading.

The organization of a club may vary slightly depending on the target group, but the basic principles described in this chapter and the materials presented in other chapters will still work with each of these groups. Thoughtful planning will make your club successful.

PLANNING

In planning your book club some issues need to be addressed.

Who are your target participants? Each of the possible target groups (parents, teachers, students) may affect other planning choices, such as meeting times.

Where should the meetings be held? Your site should be centrally located and convenient. We selected our school library.

What is the best time for your club to meet? That depends on your target group. Working parents might find early evening or Saturday morning convenient. If teachers and students are included, after school might be better. Our group met first thing on Wednesday mornings. Involve your parents' association if they are active.

How long should the meetings last? Our meetings lasted about an hour and 15 minutes, which was about all the time we could spare from our regular schedule.

How often should the group meet? We suggest meeting five or six times a year. A five-month schedule might include October, November, February, March, and

April. The sixth month could be either September or May. It is usually wise to avoid the beginning of the school year and the busy time toward the end of the school year.

What topics should be discussed at meetings? This book suggests a variety of topics. Ideas for additional topics may come from the interests, comments, and needs of the club participants and their children.

MODERATOR

A book club is only as strong and dynamic as its moderators and members. Since collaboration usually strengthens any effort, look around the school and choose a fellow faculty member to assist you in organizing and moderating club meetings. Select someone with whom you would like to work and who shares your love for and commitment to reading.

The moderator should be knowledgeable about current children's literature and the topics for the particular session and be prepared to lead a discussion. He or she must be sensitive to the needs of all the members of the group and know when to change the direction or tone of the discussion. Every member of the group should be encouraged to participate and share different points of view.

For each club session, select a topic using this book as a guide. The moderators must be interested in and enthusiastic about a topic before they present it to a group. Select books with which you are familiar and which appeal to the selected audience.

We strongly recommend that the moderators of the book club be knowledgeable about the school's or district's philosophy and policies concerning library materials selection and procedures to follow in the case of challenged materials. Different parts of the country experience various levels of challenges, so it is important to follow your school's or district's policy and procedures.

It has been our experience that a book club usually alleviates and responds to a parent's concerns about the contents of children's literature. On the other hand, a parent may challenge a book on the basis of a specific section. When this happens, we recommend that the parent read the entire book and complete a challenge form. Discuss the section in question and the merits of the book with the parent in an informal meeting. If further action is required, bring the challenged material to the attention of your library advisory committee and follow other school guidelines.

Moderator's Responsibilities in Summary

1. Be familiar with the books in the topic.

2. Prepare additional discussion questions.

3. Have handouts and bibliographies—included in this book—ready for the book club meetings.

4. Know some interesting facts about the selected authors, books, and genre.

5. Include current clippings or controversial articles appropriate to present or previous topics.

6. Distribute flyers and reminders.

7. Provide necessary books.

8. Provide beverages and refreshments.

9. READ and have FUN!

MEMBERS

Let members know that they will be expected to attend meetings, be on time, and be considerate of other participants and their opinions. They should read the books for each topic and participate in discussion. Members should share books and information with others and be alert for additional articles, ideas, and suggestions to share with the group.

Members' Responsibilities in Summary

1. Take notes as you read.

2. Respond to the guided reading questions.

3. Share your feelings and experiences.

4. Read a book to a child.

5. Attend meetings and be an active participant.

6. READ and have FUN!

PUBLICITY

How do you get the word out about your new club? Select meeting dates ahead of time so that they can be included in the school calendar and the information can be included in parents' association information. Advertise throughout the school and announce the program at Open House and the first parents' association meeting. Send invitations to prospective club members. If the group is small at first, do not be discouraged; the word will spread and the group will grow.

Once your club is active, group members can be your greatest advocates and allies. Ask them to invite friends who can benefit from the meetings. At the end of the year, have participants fill out a questionnaire like the one in chapter 14 of this book and use comments from it to encourage participation the next year. Testimonials confirm the usefulness of the meetings, discussion, and handouts. Your credibility as a knowledge-able resource person will be enhanced.

Typical Comments from Parents

"It is good to have guidelines when choosing books for the kids to read. Time is limited so you want them to read worthwhile books."

"The handouts were excellent, very helpful for future use."

"It was a wonderful year of meetings."

"The meetings were informative. I also enjoyed the camaraderie of meeting other parents who were interested in reading and education. I enjoyed familiarizing myself with the quality books available to my children."

PREPARATION

What about the first topic? Select one of the sessions suggested in this text that you like and are enthusiastic about. We usually started our club in October and began with "Horror for Kids." This topic was timely and generated a great deal of interest and curiosity.

How do you get books to the parents? For the first session, we set aside books in the library three weeks in advance for the topic we had chosen. We notified the parents that they could come and check out the books they would like to read. Alternatively, we would select some books and send them home with the member's children. This procedure is necessary only for the first meeting. Thereafter, books for the next topic are made available at the end of every session. Thus, the books discussed at a particular meeting are returned and exchanged for books on the next topic. Often, parents also checked out different books on the topic just discussed, as well as books on the new topic.

For various sessions, you may choose to have all participants read the same book or different books on the same topic. Each approach has its advantages. When everyone reads the same book, the discussion is usually better. We especially recommend this approach with a controversial book. When participants read different books in the same topic area, the discussion is broader and usually generates further interest in other books among the participants. We recommend this approach with such topics as poetry and nonfiction.

What happens at the initial meeting? At the first meeting, provide name tags and have everyone including the moderators introduce themselves. Briefly describe the club's purposes and benefits. Provide beverages and refreshments in an informal atmosphere. Push tables together or form a circle. Keep it light and fun.

PROCESS

What is the format of the meetings? The moderators should see that all members participate. After a quick update on the previous session, introduce the topic for the present session. Ask each member to comment on the books just read. Usually this is all that is needed, but have some questions ready in case of a lull. Draw out those members who tend to sit back; do not allow any one member to dominate the discussion.

Highlight some books in the bibliographies included in this book and choose titles that are appropriate for your group. Distribute handouts at the beginning of your meeting. These might include the overview, annotated journal articles, annotated bibliography, and bibliography. After summarizing the present topic, close the session with a brief introduction to the next topic, preview a few books, and hand out the guided reading questions.

ACQUISITION OF BOOKS

How can you obtain the books needed for your book club? There are many ways to acquire books. The following ideas were used to enhance our library and classroom collections.

Library Gift Book Program

At the beginning of the school year, send or hand out a general flyer explaining the gift book program to all parents. Interested parents make a specified donation to the library; the donor's child or honoree is recognized by being the first to take out the gift book. The funds generated cover the cost of the entire program, including preselected books and stationery. A bookplate is placed in the book to mark the occasion. The honored person is given a bookmark inscribed with his or her name and the occasion, as a reminder of the donated book.

Possible occasions for donating books are numerous. We have even had a book donated in honor of a new family member—a puppy! Some suggestions include:

In Memory of . . .

Have a Great School Year

Congratulations on a Good Year

Happy Valentine's Day—I love you! (for these, a small red heart was affixed to the bookplate and bookmark)

To a Special Teacher

Merry Christmas

Happy Hanukkah

This is a very successful program. Solicit two or three reliable parents from the parents' association to organize and supervise the mailings and paperwork.

Bookshare Book Fair

The Bookshare Book Fair runs like any other book fair, except that students and parents provide the books sold. Three weeks prior to the book fair, students bring in books they no longer want or have outgrown. Books are sorted by age group and checked for appropriateness. The library takes first pick of the books to select those that would enhance the school's collection. The fair is open to the school community for the first three days. The fair is held in the library, and all books are sold for 50 cents each, regardless of whether they are paperback or hardcover.

We hold this function twice a year, once in the fall and once in the spring. The biggest problem we have is storing the books prior to the book fair. Because we tend to receive a large number of books for young children, we specifically invite the local nursery schools to come on the fourth day of the book fair. Unsold books are either saved for the next book fair or donated to appropriate local charities. This worthwhile program enhances the library's collection and places recycled books in the hands of many, many children.

School Book Clubs

School book clubs are another source of less expensive books and are worth the recordkeeping. If you are concerned that some of your children are unable to purchase books, try using your bonus points for extra books. These clubs are a good source for multiple copies of a particular book or a set of books that can be discussed at sessions of your own book club and then used in classrooms.

Civic Organizations

Identify community sponsors and civic groups for grant money or donations. Some organizations to consider are Kiwanis, Junior League, Rotary, public libraries, local businesses, neighborhood associations, and your school parents' association. A letter or a personal visit from the moderators may be most effective. Let the organizations know that their support will be gratefully acknowledged on all handouts.

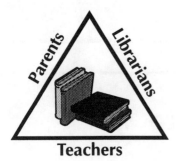

Parents
Librarians
Teachers

Chapter 2

Sure Hits to Read Aloud

OVERVIEW

Reading aloud to children not only builds their language skills and imaginations, but also brings families closer together. It affords the parent an opportunity to share and discuss a variety of interests, literature, and authors. Reading aloud demonstrates the connections between oral and written language. So, cuddle up! Reading aloud is fun and fosters lifelong reading habits.

Read-aloud books should be appealing to the adult while stretching the mind and imagination of the child. The best stories allow readers to draw their own conclusions, have a fast-paced plot, and contain easy-to-read dialogue. Soon you will have old and new favorites.

After picking a daily time to read, avoid all interruptions. Talk about the author, title, or illustrations before you begin. As you read, be expressive with your voice and discuss words and their meanings as you encounter them. Try to predict what will happen in the story and relate the events to the child's background knowledge.

GUIDED READING QUESTIONS

1. Between now and the next session, set aside 20 to 30 uninterrupted minutes each day to spend reading to your children. After a while, do you notice any changes in attitudes or behavior during this time?

2. Read a title from the bibliography and a selection from *Hey! Listen to This* or *Read All About It!* by Jim Trelease.

3. Ask open-ended questions to encourage your children to think about what they are hearing.

4. Look for favorite lines or short passages and share these lines again at the next reading session.

5. Involve different members of the family in your read-aloud sessions (Dad, older brothers or sisters, grandparents).

6. Be prepared to share your successes and disappointments with the rest of the group. Will you continue with read-aloud sessions?

JOURNAL ARTICLE

Mommy! Daddy! Read to Me!

Librarians—public and school—team to create new readers
by taking time with their parents.

Imagine this scenario. A group of 20 interested mothers and fathers who have committed an hour a week for the next four weeks at your library. They've come to hear how they can improve their parenting skills by reading to their children and listening to their children read to them.

Imagine also that these parents are not distracted by their children because the children are also engaged in activities.

At various times over recent years, Mary Ann Gilpatrick, youth services librarian at Walla Walla (WA) Public Library, Shirley Rodenberg, library media specialist at Blue Ridge Elementary School, and I discussed the provision of a parents' workshop focused on reading to children. All of us believe that one of the best guarantees of reading success is having an adult read to a child from birth to school age. But we also felt that significant numbers of parents in the community did not have the necessary skills to read to their children. Therefore we proposed a workshop at which parents would learn the skills needed to become successful at reading aloud.

By Allen Kopf. Reprinted with permission from *School Library Journal* (March 1995), page 150. Allen Kopf is supervisor, library, media, and technology services at Walla Walla, WA, Public Schools.

What We Wanted to Give Parents

Before we started planning, we knew we wanted to concentrate on two skill areas. First, we wanted parents to learn how to nurture children as they listen to stories, i.e., the parent sits close to the child in a chair. Second, we wanted them to read in an appropriate way, i.e., the parent demonstrates that print is read from left to right.

We also wanted the workshop to encourage reading awareness in the home, to help parents learn how to provide children with language enrichment activities, and to build parent support through follow-up and continuing contacts.

We recognized that many of the parents being targeted for the workshop do not have books at home. And while they have access to the public library, we know that transportation problems and a lack of awareness about what is available keep parents from using it. Part of our mission, then, was to introduce them to the public library. We also planned to teach parents how to select books, and invited them to check out materials at the school library media center.

Creating a Road Map

Early in 1993, we took two days away from phones to plan our Parents and Kids Reading Together Workshop on the campus of central Washington University in Ellensburg.

That summer, we were awarded a $9,500 Chapter 2 "20 Percent" Innovative Projects of Statewide Significance Grant through the office of the superintendent. We spent $5,000 on books for parents and kids, $1,600 on parenting videotapes, and $100 for print materials to teach parents how to use the library, choose good books, and read to their children. We used the remainder—$2,800—for stipends to pay those running the workshop.

The Main Event

In the fall, we introduced the first Parents and Kids Reading Together Workshop at Blue Ridge Elementary School. Twenty-three families were accepted and approximately 15 families came each week, some with both mother and father. About 50 percent were Hispanic. Before the workshop started, Juanita Gillum, the kindergarten home visitor, told parents about the workshop and took applications to them. Undoubtedly she was responsible for the good turnout of Hispanic parents.

Joanne Reiter, school staff development assistant for Walla Walla Public Schools, taught the parents' workshop at the library media center with assistance from Manuel Armenta, a bilingual teaching assistant. They modeled reading-aloud techniques, shared examples of books to be read to children, and taught parents about the reading process.

The rest of us ran the children's portion of the workshop, dividing it into two parts: music and storytelling. The children attended both parts, divided by age into two groups that switched midway through the evening. For the youngest children we provided child care. At the end of the evening, the children joined their parents in the library and chose books to take home.

During the fifth week, we took parents and children to the Walla Walla Public Library. Gilpatrick gave a tour of the library and taught parents how to use the online catalog. The library issued eight new cards to parents during the course of the evening.

Valuable Enough to Offer Again

We all feel that the workshop was very successful and that we met our goals and objectives. In their evaluations, parents reported reading about 10 books on average per week with their children. Rodenberg reports that weeks after the program ended parents were still coming to the library media center. As a result, we plan to offer the workshop again, and plans are being developed to start the program at other schools in the district.

If you would like additional information about Parents and Kids Reading Together Workshop, please contact me at Walla Walla Public Schools, 364 S. Park St., Walla Walla, WA 99362-3293. ▲

ANNOTATED JOURNAL ARTICLES

Freeman, Judy. "Reading Aloud: A Few Tricks of the Trade," *School Library Journal* (July 1992): 26-29.

A good article to share with fellow teachers and parents. It includes tips on how to read to children and the benefits of reading aloud. The author cautions against asking too many questions. Questions should be broad-based. They should challenge the students to identify with the character and to think about what can be applied to their own situations. Professional educators are most responsible for instilling in students the fun and joy of reading. "Reading aloud is the most potent way to influence children to become readers themselves."

Mazzoco, Michele. "The Magic of Reading Aloud," *Journal of Youth Services in Libraries* (Spring 1993): 312-14.

While participating in the Denver Public Library Read-Aloud Program, Mazzoco witnessed two styles of reading aloud. "The first style seemed to reflect to me the enthusiasm for the child as listener as well as for the book being read. . . . The second style focused primarily on the story rather than the child." The reader did not respond to child-initiated discussion but remained fixed on the story. The second style was promoted, and after a few weeks, fewer interruptions occurred and the young children were better able to sit through a number of books. Interactions between children and reader occurred, but they occurred before and after—not during—the story.

Moss, Barbara. "Using Children's Nonfiction Tradebooks as Read-Alouds," *Language Arts* (February 1995): 122-25.

Teachers chose high-quality fantasy and realistic fiction as read-alouds. They often neglect nonfiction because in the past, a great deal of nonfiction was of mediocre quality and children had little interest in this genre. This article shows how nonfiction has improved and how nonfiction read-alouds can enrich children's learning experiences.

Schwartz, David M. "Most Important Thing You Can Do for Your Child" (adapted from *Smithsonian,* February 1995), *Reader's Digest* (July 1995): 163-64.

This article should be shared with all parents and teachers. Jim Trelease, featured in this article, discusses the importance of reading aloud to children. It is as important as a hug. He claims that too many children associate reading with work. It is our duty to teach children to want to read.

Young, Petey. "Amazing What Can Happen When You Read to Them," *Journal of Reading* (October 1991): 148-49.

One is never too old to be read to. Young, a college professor, reads *James and the Giant Peach* to future high school teachers. "When reading aloud, I stop in midsentence and begin the day's work without reference to or explanation of the reading." At the end of the course, she asks her students to complete the following three statements: "I think the reason Petey reads in high school methods class is _____ . My personal reaction to it is _____ . If she is going to read, the kind of thing I would like her to read about would be _____ ."

ANNOTATED BIBLIOGRAPHY

Alexander, Lloyd. *The Fortune-Tellers*. Dutton Children's Books, 1992.

A young carpenter who wanted to know his future visited an elderly fortune-teller. On his way home, he began to think of more questions to ask the fortune-teller. When he returned, the fortune-teller was gone and the landlord thought she had witnessed a miracle—the elderly fortune teller was now young. What would the young fortune-teller's future bring?

Byars, Betsy. *The Pinballs.* Harper & Row, 1977.

Two boys and a girl living in a foster home refer to themselves as *pinballs,* because they have no control over where they settle. They learn to care about themselves and each other.

Fleischman, Sid. *The Whipping Boy.* Greenwillow Books, 1986.

Because it was forbidden to whip, spank, or whack the royal prince, the orphan Jemmy-From-The-Streets was forced to serve as Prince Brat's whipping boy. This meant Jemmy was kept in the castle to be punished in place of the Prince. One night, the Prince made Jemmy run away with him. They met two scoundrels, Hold-Your-Nose Billy and Cutwater. After discovering who the young lads were, the outlaws decided that Jemmy was the Royal Highness and forced him to write a ransom note. Thanks to Jemmy, the Prince returned home safely, and Jemmy was placed under the Prince's protection.

Gardiner, John Reynolds. *Stone Fox.* Thomas Y. Crowell, 1980.

This wonderful story of a boy and his dog is based on a Rocky Mountain legend. Willy's grandfather is ill, and Willy must keep the farm going. How will he raise the $500 needed to pay off the delinquent back taxes? His only hope is to compete against the best dogsled racers in the country and win the big prize money.

Henkes, Kevin. *Chrysanthemum.* Greenwillow Books, 1991.

What is it like to be named after a flower? Chrysanthemum loved her name until she started school. When Chrysanthemum's name was called at roll call, everyone giggled. That was the start of miserable days until she met Mrs. Twinkle, the music teacher.

Herzig, Alison Cragin. *Mystery on October Road.* Viking, 1991.

Catherine Cooney's new neighbor wore a bandanna over his face and a hat pulled down over his eyes. He looked like a villain in a Western movie. Encouraged by her friends, Catherine opens his basement window and drops hard to the floor. Hearing a van arrive, she tries to climb out of the basement, falls, and is unable to walk. She is caught and soon learns her neighbor's secret.

BIBLIOGRAPHY

Primary

Aylesworth, Jim. *Old Black Fly.* Henry Holt, 1992.

Barrett, Judith. *Cloudy with a Chance of Meatballs.* Atheneum, 1982.

Brett, Jan. *Berlioz the Bear.* G. P. Putnam's Sons, 1991.

Brown, Marc. *Arthur Meets the President.* Little, Brown, 1991.

Cherry, Lynne. *The Great Kapok Tree: A Tale of the Amazon Rain Forest.* Harcourt Brace Jovanovich, 1990.

Cooney, Barbara. *Miss Rumphius.* Viking, 1982.

dePaola, Tomie. *Tom.* G. P. Putnam's Sons, 1993.

Devlin, Wende, and Harry Devlin. *Cranberry Thanksgiving.* Four Winds Press, 1971.

Gackenbach, Dick. *Harry and the Terrible Whatzit.* Houghton Mifflin, 1977.

Henkes, Kevin. *Julius, the Baby of the World.* Greenwillow Books, 1990.

Hoffman, Mary. *Amazing Grace.* Dial Books for Young Readers, 1991.

Hopkinson, Deborah. *Sweet Clara and the Freedom Quilt.* Alfred A. Knopf, 1993.

Kellogg, Stephen. *The Island of the Skog.* Houghton Mifflin, 1975.

Leaf, Munro. *The Story of Ferdinand.* Viking, 1936.

Lionni, Leo. *Matthew's Dream.* Alfred A. Knopf, 1991.

Lobel, Arnold. *Frog and Toad Are Friends.* Harper & Row, 1970.

Marshall, James. *The Cut-Ups Cut Loose.* Viking, 1987.

Parish, Peggy. *Amelia Bedelia.* Harper & Row, 1963.

Polacco, Patricia. *Babushka's Doll.* Simon & Schuster, 1990.

———. *Just Plain Fancy.* Bantam Books, 1990.

———. *Thunder Cake.* Philomel, 1990.

Potter, Beatrix. *The Tale of Peter Rabbit.* Dover, 1972.

Ringgold, Faith. *Tar Beach.* Crown, 1991.

Scieszka, Jon. *The Frog Prince Continued.* Viking, 1991.

———. *The True Story of the 3 Little Pigs by A. Wolf.* Viking, 1989.

Steig, William. *Brave Irene.* Farrar, Straus & Giroux, 1988.

Waber, Bernard. *The House on East 89th Street.* Houghton Mifflin, 1975.

Ward, Lynd. *The Biggest Bear.* Houghton Mifflin, 1973.

Williams, Vera B. *A Chair for My Mother.* Greenwillow Books, 1982.

Yolen, Jane. *Owl Moon.* Philomel, 1987.

General Fiction

Atwater, Richard, and Florence Atwater. *Mr. Popper's Penguins.* Little, Brown, 1938.

Babbit, Natalie. *Tuck Everlasting.* Farrar, Straus & Giroux, 1986.

Banks, Lynne Reid. *The Indian in the Cupboard.* Doubleday, 1981.

Bauer, Marion Dane. *On My Honor.* Dell, 1987.

———. *Rain of Fire.* Clarion Books, 1983.

Blume, Judy. *Tales of a Fourth Grade Nothing.* Dell, 1972.

Bulla, Clyde. *A Lion to Guard Us.* Thomas Y. Crowell, 1981.

Bunting, Eve. *Someone Is Hiding on Alcatraz Island.* Clarion Books, 1984.

Burnett, Frances Hodgson. *The Secret Garden.* Viking, 1989.

Byars, Betsy. *The Midnight Fox.* Viking, 1968.

———. *The Pinballs.* Harper & Row, 1977.

Cameron, Ann. *The Stories Julian Tells.* Pantheon, 1987.

Catling, Patrick Skene. *The Chocolate Touch.* Bantam Books, 1988.

Cleary, Beverly. *Ramona the Pest.* Dell, 1968.

Clifford, Eth. *Help! I'm a Prisoner in the Library.* Scholastic, 1985.

Cohen, Barbara. *Thank You, Jackie Robinson.* Lothrop, Lee & Shepard, 1986.

Collier, James L., and Christopher Collier. *Jump Ship to Freedom.* Delacorte Press, 1981.

Collodi, Carlo. *The Adventures of Pinocchio.* Childrens Press, 1968.

Dahl, Roald. *Danny the Champion of the World.* Alfred A. Knopf, 1975.

————. *Fantastic Mr. Fox.* Puffin Books, 1988.

Dalgliesh, Alice. *The Courage of Sarah Noble.* Macmillan, 1986.

Estes, Eleanor. *The Hundred Dresses.* Harcourt Brace Jovanovich, 1974.

Fleischman, Sid. *The Whipping Boy.* Greenwillow Books, 1986.

Gardiner, John R. *The Stone Fox.* Thomas Y. Crowell, 1980.

George, Jean. *My Side of the Mountain.* E. P. Dutton, 1975.

Konigsburg, E. L. *From the Mixed-Up Files of Mrs. Basil E. Frankweiler.* Atheneum, 1973.

London, Jack. *The Call of the Wild.* Macmillan, 1963.

Lord, Bette Bao. *In the Year of the Boar and Jackie Robinson.* Harper & Row, 1986.

McCloskey, Robert. *Homer Price.* Viking, 1943.

Morey, Walt. *Gentle Ben.* E. P. Dutton, 1965.

Mowat, Farley. *Owls in the Family.* Little, Brown, 1961.

O'Brien, Robert C. *Mrs. Frisby and the Rats of NIMH.* Atheneum, 1971.

O'Dell, Scott. *Sarah Bishop.* Houghton Mifflin, 1980.

Park, Barbara. *Skinnybones.* Alfred A. Knopf, 1982.

Paulsen, Gary. *Hatchet.* Bradbury Press, 1987.

Peck, Robert Newton. *Soup.* Alfred A. Knopf, 1974.

Peterson, John. *The Littles.* Scholastic, 1970.

Roberts, Willo Davis. *The Girl with the Silver Eyes.* Atheneum, 1980.

Robinson, Barbara. *The Best Christmas Pageant Ever.* Harper & Row, 1972.

Sachar, Louis. *Wayside School Is Falling Down.* Lothrop, Lee & Shepard, 1989.

Smith, Robert K. *Chocolate Fever.* Putnam, 1989.

Speare, Elizabeth George. *The Sign of the Beaver.* Houghton Mifflin, 1983.

Sperry, Armstrong. *Call It Courage.* Macmillan, 1940.

Taylor, Mildred. *Roll of Thunder, Hear My Cry.* Dial Press, 1976.

Taylor, Theodore. *The Cay.* Doubleday, 1969.

Wallace, Bill. *A Dog Called Kitty.* Holiday House, 1980.

White, E. B. *Charlotte's Web.* Harper & Row, 1952.

Williams, Margery. *The Velveteen Rabbit.* Alfred A. Knopf, 1985.

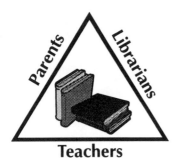

Parents · Librarians · Teachers

Chapter 3

Horror for Kids

OVERVIEW

Sales are booming in this genre for kids; horror novels are popular with young readers. They are favorites because this is one way for youngsters to enjoy the excitement of being terrified while still being in control. Children like the aggression and fear in books crammed with murder, mystery, and mayhem. These books were originally targeted by publishers at children ages 12 and older, but they are actually being read by much younger readers.

Noting the increased popularity of these books, publishers have produced new, scary covers for previously released books to enhance sales. Some authors are trying to outdo others to generate sales by using increasingly violent plots filled with psychotic killers and bloody murders.

These books are now being marketed to younger and younger age groups. This new genre motivates reading, and there is no need for alarm unless a child reads only these books and has no other interests or seems anxious and begins having nightmares. It is best not to censor or forbid these books. Parents should read some of the books themselves so that they can discuss the stories or at least answer questions. During book club sessions they may find some alternative titles or authors to recommend to their children.

GUIDED READING QUESTIONS

1. Compare the covers of the books you read. Are they frightening? If so, to which age group?

2. Would both boys and girls find the books appealing?

3. How do you feel about your son or daughter reading these books?

4. Was the story a good mystery? Did it have a plot? Were the characters developed?

5. Did you like the way adults were portrayed in the books?

6. Did anything objectionable happen in the books?

Books That Go Bump in the Night

Several new paperback series provide thrills and chills for middle-grade readers.

David Weiss, age nine, a recent devotee of horror novels, sounds as thrilled about his chosen genre as those who publish it.

"It all started last November," the New York City fourth-grader explains. "I didn't really like to read" until two books, one about Dracula and another about a vampire, stirred his imagination. "I read them over and over again," he says, "and now I only like reading because of horror."

The power of spine-tingling tales to lure young adult readers is well-documented by the amazing popularity of authors like Christopher Pike, and series like R. L. Stine's Fear Street (Pocket). But only in the past year have publishers found that the appeal of scary stories is casting its spell on the younger set. Beginning with Stine's Goosebumps, which Scholastic began last July, there has been a veritable bumper crop of horror series aimed at middle-graders: the Foul Play series from Puffin, which began in time for last Halloween; Harper Trophy Chillers, which launched last fall; and Shockers from Grossett & Dunlap, which entered the market in June. For fall '93, Random House has announced two middle-grade series as well.

The remarkable success of books for the 8-to-12 set such as the Babysitters Club and Sweet Valley Twins encouraged publishers to think in terms of series, but it was the trickle-down from the YA market that drew their attention to horror. "When the kids who are writing you letters about one series are younger than the target age, you have a pretty good hunch there's a new market out there," says Jean Feiwel, publisher at Scholastic, who developed the Goosebumps series after watching the response from younger readers to Stine's YA books.

"What we realized was that at a certain age, kids jump to Stephen King," comments Craig Walker, v-p and editor-in-chief at Grossett & Dunlap. "That leaves a whole section of that market unserviced by juvenile publishers. We're trying to capture them *pre*-Stephen King." Put simply, he says, "We're niche publishing in the horror genre."

And niche publishing, as the Babysitters Club so dramatically proved, can have its rewards. Goosebumps has been the most striking success in middle-grade horror so far, and a beacon to other publishers. With eerie but colorful cover illustrations, the tales of children confronting supernatural situations are making R. L. Stine as much of a cult celebrity as Ann Martin. According to Feiwel, bimonthly print runs of the books began at 30,000; now Scholastic is publishing a new book each month with initial print runs of 100,000. This month marked the appearance of the 10th book in the series.

By M. P. Dunleavey. Reprinted with permission from *Publishers Weekly* (July 5, 1993), page 30. Dunleavey is a freelance journalist who writes frequently for *PW*, the *New York Times*, and various environmental magazines.

Tisha Hamilton, editor of Puffin's four Foul Play books by John Peel, says that print runs are holding steady at 35,000 and sales are "okay, not boffo." Grossett & Dunlap sprung Shockers (also by John Peel) on the market last month with an initial print run of 50,000 for each of its four books. Lisa Banim, senior editor of the Random House Bullseye line, which includes Bullseye Chillers and the Shadow Zone, says their commitment is roughly the same for each, though she declined to release the figures.

The Price Is Right

Though priced comparably (from about $2.95 to $3.95) to appeal to readers who may be dipping into their own pockets, each series has its own personality and reason for being, which makes this niche a bit like a race being run half a dozen different ways.

Feiwel attributes the popularity of Goosebumps to the special touch of Stine, who was a magazine editor at Scholastic for many years before writing his first YA novel. In addition to his series work, Stine now writes for the children's TV network Nickelodeon.

"The key thing here is you can identify the category you want to publish to, but then you have to marry it to the right person," Feiwel says. "Then, you have to have the right packaging and the right timing."

Parachute Press, the book packager that developed the series title for Goosebumps, played an important role in concocting the idea for a middle-grade horror series, Feiwel says, but she stresses the importance of a single, guiding author to shape the series. "It means someone behind it has a vision, a kind of commitment and creative involvement."

The Foul Play series, on the other hand, until now written by John Peel, will begin highlighting a range of writers for future books. Hamilton says the series, which is based on the concept of children's games turned deadly—*Tag (You're Dead)* is one, *Hangman* another—relies on a team of writers to enrich the series rather than a single voice. The next featured writer is Robin Hardy, a former writer for the Hardy Boys books.

Hamilton adds that the series idea was brought to them by Chardiet Unlimited, a book packager, which continues to collaborate on the books. "It's a 50-50 effort," Hamilton says.

Banim at Random House says they are trying to give children something completely different from other horror series. Bullseye Chillers is a repackaging of classic horror stories targeted to a somewhat younger (7-11) market. *Frankenstein* and *Phantom of the Opera* are being published in August, accompanied by two originals in the same gothic style.

The Shadow Zone, Banim says, "is for the standard 8-to-12 age group"; it was developed in conjunction with packager Twelve House Productions. Borrowing from the *Twilight Zone* concept, these stories involved "ordinary kids who suddenly find themselves in the Shadow Zone" where strange things happen. Their key feature is humor, she says. "The books are not true horror. They get a little icky, but they're low-key, not frightening."

Taking a similar approach is Pocket Books' Minstrel imprint ("We like to serve up our horror with a little twist of humor," says marketing director Nancy Pines). Minstrel has several middle-grade horror series and stand-alone titles; the most successful have been Bruce Coville's My Teacher quartet, which has sold in excess of two million copies total; and Ann Hodgman's My Babysitter books.

Coming at the market from yet another direction are the HarperTrophy Chillers. "We're more of a trade approach to horror," says editor Ginee Seo. Trophy Chillers publishes one book per season, often a collection of stories or a reprint (though originals are featured as well), and Seo says they are in no rush to produce the sort of series that everyone else has.

Goosebumps, Foul Play, Trophy Chillers, Bullseye Chillers and Shadow Zone are targeted at boys as well as girls, and offer thrills and chills without the gore, but Grossett & Dunlap's Shockers were designed to come a little closer to adult horror in order to attract boys. "Girls will read it no matter what, if it appeals to them," Craig Walker points out. "But boys have been left out of the horror market."

Issued in rack size, with more sophisticated, less cartoony cover illustrations than the other series, Shockers features boys being threatened and sometimes overcome by supernatural forces. "They're based on the classic icons of horror," Walker says. Vampires, werewolves, ghosts and aliens haunt the first four Shockers titles, but unlike other books that offer a soothing ending, these stories conclude with more open-ended twists. In *Alien Prey*, for example, four friends fighting alien beings find that one among them is the alien they fear.

Hooked on Horror

For now there is no end in sight for the middle-grade horror market, but publishers say at least one unexpected goal has been achieved: an age group that has far fewer books to choose from, relative to when they were younger, is getting more of the variety it deserves. Feedback from children, parents and teachers is that the right touch can bring out bookworms in any market, and now, especially for boys who are so often disenchanted with reading, horror is doing the job.

Young readers like David are responding enthusiastically. "In your imagination, anything can happen," he says. "You can die, you can live. You're taken somewhere out of reality—to fantasy." And for all the children discovering the powerful pleasure of fantasy thanks to scary stories designed just for them, there are plenty more where that came from. ▲

ANNOTATED JOURNAL ARTICLES

Alderdice, Kit. "R. L. Stine: 90 Million Spooky Adventures," *Publishers Weekly* (July 1995): 208-9.

The Fear Street series marked the first time horror novels were done as a series using one location (Shadyside). There are some recurring background characters, but each book has a new protagonist. The best part of all this, according to Stine, is that both Fear Street and Goosebumps are avidly read by both boys and girls. Boys, if they read at all, usually read nonfiction and biographies. The article describes how Stine writes two books a month, and that he has a contract for three more years of these books!

Campbell, Patty. "The Sand in the Oyster," *Horn Book Magazine* (March-April 1994): 234-35.

The popularity of the horror genre is due to marketing, compelling stories, and predictable formulas, dealing with rejection and life after death. Teens say they want to be able to read trashy books—they get enough classics in school. Serious YA authors report pressure from publishers to write in the horror mode because the bottom line is that these books sell.

Gray, Paul. "Carnage: An Open Book," *Time* (August 1993): 54.

This article describes the increasing popularity of the new thriller genre for teenagers. The books are loaded with violence and gore. Short chapters with suspense endings keep teens with limited attention spans turning pages. The authors claim that their books are all in good fun and not nearly as scary as the real world.

Kies, Cosette. "EEEK! They Just Keep Coming! YA Horror Series," *VOYA* (April 1994): 17-19.

Publishers have announced plans to increase the number of teen horror titles. The presence of adults in these stories is kept to a minimum. The stories are predictable, with casual use of the supernatural, some humor, and simple plots. The new market attracts an even younger audience, and newer horror books tend not to list reading interest or grade level anywhere on the book. It is obvious that these books are written quickly to sell big. They are not great literature, but kids are reading them.

Tucker, Ken. "Nameless Fear Stalks the Middle-Class Teenager: Perhaps It Is the Fear of Boredom," *New York Times Book Review* (November 1993): 27.

These stories are set in normal surroundings: schools, shopping malls, middle-class neighborhoods. The main characters are involved in normal activities: sleeping away at camp, volunteering at the hospital, or going off to college. The agents of menace are authority figures gone mad: doctors, teachers, a best friend's mom or dad. The stories are filled with helpless girls, vulgar pranks, and characters with lackluster personalities. They are obviously assembly-line products. The lesson to be learned, according to Tucker, is that "[w]e have less to fear from the hacksaw than from the hacks."

BIBLIOGRAPHY

Alphin, Elaine M. *The Ghost Cadet*. Henry Holt, 1991.

Avi. *Something Upstairs: Tale of Ghosts*. Orchard, 1988.

Bellairs, John. *The Dark Secret of Weatherend*. Bantam Books, 1984.

Bunting, Eve. *Night of the Gargoyles*. Clarion Books, 1994.

———. *Someone Is Hiding on Alcatraz Island*. Clarion Books, 1984.

Byars, Betsy. *McMummy*. Viking, 1993.

Cassedy, Sylvia. *Behind the Attic Wall*. Thomas Y. Crowell, 1983.

Cecil, Laura, ed. *Boo! Stories to Make You Jump*. Greenwillow Books, 1990.

Duncan, Lois. *I Know What You Did Last Summer*. Archway Paper, 1973.

Emberley, Ed. *Go Away, Big Green Monster*. Little, Brown, 1993.

George, Jean Craighead. *The Fire Bug Connection*. HarperCollins, 1993.

Hahn, Mary Downing. *Wait Till Helen Comes*. Clarion Books, 1986.

Hamilton, Virginia. *The Dark Way: Stories from the Spirit*. Harcourt Brace Jovanovich, 1990.

———. *The House of Dies Drear*. Macmillan, 1984.

Hilgartner, Beth. *A Murder for Her Majesty*. Houghton Mifflin, 1986.

Howe, James. *Scared Silly*. Avon Books, 1989.

Impey, Rose. *Scare Yourself to Sleep*. Dell, 1988.

Macguire, Gregory. *Seven Spiders Spinning*. Clarion Books, 1994.

Macklin, John. *World's Strangest "True" Ghost Stories*. Sterling, 1990.

Mahy, Margaret. *The Haunting*. Macmillan, 1982.

Naylor, Phyllis Reynolds. *The Witch Returns*. Dell, 1992.

Nixon, Joan Lowry. *Secret Silent Screams*. Laurel Leaf, 1988.

San Souci, Robert D. *Short and Shivery: Thirty Chilling Tales*. Doubleday, 1987.

Schwartz, Alvin. *Scary Stories to Tell in the Dark*. HarperCollins, 1981.

———. *Scary Stories 3: More Tales to Chill Your Bones*. HarperCollins, 1991.

Snyder, Zilpha Keatley. *The Headless Cupid*. Macmillan, 1971.

———. *13 Tales of Horror*. Scholastic, 1991.

Turner, Ann. *Rosemary's Witch*. HarperCollins, 1991.

Wallace, Bill. *Blackwater Swamp*. Holiday House, 1994.

———. *Trapped in Death Cave*. Holiday House, 1984.

Wright, Betty Ren. *The Dollhouse Murders*. Scholastic, 1983.

———. *The Ghost Came Calling*. Scholastic, 1994.

BIBLIOGRAPHY OF POPULAR AUTHORS AND SERIES

Following is a list of some of the many horror/thriller series that are available for intermediate and young adults. This is not a complete compilation. The number of books in the series is the authors' best accounting as of June 1996. R. L. Stine is the most popular and regularly has eight of the ten spots on *Publishers Weekly*'s children's bestsellers list.

Hoh, Diane
  Nightmare Hall. Scholastic. Young Adult. 20 titles.
  "High on a hillside overlooking Salem University hidden in shadows and shrouded in silence sits Nightmare Hall. Nightmare Hall, the students call it. Because that is where the terror began." This quotation, taken from the back cover, gains one's attention immediately.

Packard, Edward
Choose Your Own Nightmare. Bantam. Intermediate. 1 title.
A new series based on the choose-your-own-adventure platform. You control the twists and turns, you control your own nightmare.

Pike, Christopher
Archway. 25 titles.
Spooksville. Pocket Books. Young Adult. 7 titles.
In 1994, Christopher Pike was the top YA horror author, and his books are not tied to only one series. Prior to writing, Pike painted houses, worked in a factory, and programmed computers. He has several hobbies. His favorite is making sure his books are prominently displayed in local bookstores. Pike's books generally are listed for a slightly older age group because they may contain sex rather than romance as in other horror series.

Rice, Bebe Faas
Doomsday Mall. Bantam. Intermediate. 5 titles.
This series is set in malls, where kids love to hang out, which are packed, and where evil awaits.

Stine, R. L.
The Cataluna Chronicles. Archway. Young Adult. 2 titles.
Fear Street. Archway. Young Adult. 36 titles.
Fear Street Cheerleaders. Archway. Young Adult. 3 titles.
Fear Street Saga. Archway. Young Adult. 3 titles.
Fear Street Super Chillers. Archway. Young Adult. 10 titles.
99 Fear Street: The House of Evil. Archway. Young Adult. 3 titles.
Goosebumps. Scholastic. Intermediate. 45 titles.
R. L. Stine switched from writing humorous stories to horror in 1985. Over a million copies of his books are sold every month. One can watch a Goosebumps television series, join a fan club, or locate information about Stine and his books on the World Wide Web. Stine believes that children enjoy being scared, and it appears he is making the most of it. Adults seem to accept these books with a certain reluctance and with the pessimistic thought that "at least they are reading something."

Other Major Publishers' Series

Grossett and Dunlap's Shockers

HarperTrophy Chillers

Puffin's Foul Play

Random House Bullseye Chillers and Shadow Zone

Scholastic Point Thriller

Starfire Horror

There is no end in sight for the middle-grade horror market and its appeal to girls as well as boys. This listing shows the variety and number of publishers getting into this lucrative market.

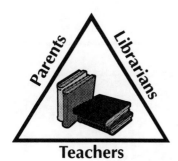

Teachers

Chapter 4

Historical Fiction

OVERVIEW

Historical fiction means a realistic tale set in the past. By reading historical novels, students can imagine themselves as part of the past and, it is hoped, increase their understanding of history. If the author is careful, the story will show how the characters existed during that time period. This is done by creating a story that grasps the reader's attention differently than a textbook. Writers like Scott O'Dell, Patricia Beatty, and Elizabeth Speare do this very well and therefore are favorites.

Historical fiction is written in two styles. One uses fictional persons and does not distinguish any specific occurrence in history. The other describes authentic people and incidents. The author should be precise and represent the time period accurately concerning dress, speech, and other styles during a particular historical period.

GUIDED READING QUESTIONS

1. Was the story realistic?

2. Were the characters fictional or actual persons?

3. Did the story accurately represent the time period?

4. Would the story hold the reader's attention differently than a textbook?

5. Will reading this story allow the student to better understand the time period and our historical heritage?

6. Did this story show how people of the past solved problems and handled mistakes?

JOURNAL ARTICLE

Imagining the Past Through Historical Novels

No matter how carefully day-to-day living has been detailed, the book will not ring true if the characters are given present-day sensibilities.

Can writers ever fully re-create the past? Probably not. They can read history books, journals, and diaries. They can study houses, furniture, and fashions. But unless they make readers feel the hopes, fears, and dreams of their characters, they have not achieved their goals. Of course, they must know the period they are writing about, and should be as historically accurate as possible, but facts and figures are the stuff of textbooks, and novels are much, much more.

When I wrote *A Promise to Keep* (Dutton, 1990), I was drawing on my own memory. I had grown up in England during World War II, and had stayed on a farm at the time of the Battle of Britain. But memory can be fickle. Was it a perfect summer? Of course not. But to 14-year-old Ellie, who was enchanted with the farm, it seemed that way at first. The story is told through her eyes, and as the summer draws to a close she comes to see the terrible waste and stupidity of war. And if my story works, YA readers will see that too.

Much of the atmosphere in that book comes from the farm setting. I had to remember that we had no electricity but used oil lamps and candles. We slept on feather

By Eileen Van Kirk. Reprinted with permission from *School Library Journal* (August 1993), page 50. Eileen Van Kirk writes fiction and nonfiction for adults and young people. She lives in Wayne, NJ.

beds. The farmer killed his own chickens, and his wife churned the butter and made the jams. Against this peaceful background, the drums of war grew ever louder, threatening bombs and an invasion. An invasion that would be announced, not by radio or television, but by the ringing of church bells all over England. Small details maybe, but by including such details, I tried to create a sense of another time and another place.

For my novel *Silk* (Berkley, 1991), set in the silk mills of Paterson, New Jersey, I had to go back beyond memory. Back to my mother's time, patching together things she and my father had told me about coming to America from England. Then I began to read, to search libraries, historical societies, museums, and, whenever possible, to talk to people who had actually worked in the mills, who remembered what it was like to work long hours for a few dollars a week. I looked at old ledgers, reports, letters. I learned how silk was thrown, reeled, carded, dyed, woven, and bought and sold.

But none of this information would have been any good if I could not capture how it felt. I had to imagine what it would be like to awaken every morning to dress in layers of petticoats, a long black skirt, lace-up boots, and cotton blouse, with little difference between summer and winter, except perhaps an extra petticoat, then walk to work and spend the next 10 hours standing by a loom, assailed by the endless, shattering racket of a mill in full spate. I could read about it, see pictures of it, even go to the museum and watch the old looms in action, but then I had to close my eyes and put myself in those lace-up boots, watch the shuttle fly back and forth, smell the soaking vats and dyes, hear the incessant noise, feel the exhaustion.

When I go to an area I plan to write about, I seldom take notes. I can always check details of streets and buildings later, but what I try to do is absorb the atmosphere. Like most of us, I was familiar with the look of Washington, D.C., but it wasn't until I walked its streets, the sun warm on my back, surrounded by the fragrance of flowering trees, that I realized in spite of its surface sophistication, Washington is, at heart, a gentle Southern city.

In European towns and cities it is still fairly easy to discover the past. Down little alleyways, in small walled sections of towns, one can easily slip back a couple of hundred years. In the States it is more difficult. We are quick to tear down, and restored sites never have quite the same aura. It is that feeling of age, that sense of another era, that writers try to capture.

But atmosphere will mean nothing if they slip in current catchwords and phrases. Television is notorious for doing this. When an antebellum heroine says she needs her space, or the hero has to go away to find himself, the illusion of a different time is shattered and the story has been brought into the present.

And no matter how carefully day-to-day living has been detailed, the book will not ring true if the characters are given present-day sensibilities. While we may strongly believe that slavery was evil, that Christianity is not the only religion, that women are equal to men, these are contemporary ideas. Protagonists can be shown to be struggling with such ideas, but they were not accepted by many.

In addition to these two caveats, today's authors have to struggle with the concept of being politically correct. In my opinion, when writing historical novels, there should be only one criterion: Are you being true to your characters and to the society in which they lived? If not, you have broken faith with readers.

One author who never falters in her understanding of time and place is Irene Hunt, whose beautiful and poignant book, *Across Five Aprils* (Berkley, 1987), is as meaningful today as it was when it was first published in 1964. It tells the story of a family torn apart by the Civil War. Jethro and Ellen Creighton are clearly living in 19th-century rural America, where hard, honest labor was the mark of a man; book learning, while cautiously respected, was not considered important; where women often worked right alongside the men in the fields, but were still solely responsible for the household chores, and would not have been able to conceive of a different order.

Within this framework Hunt describes a warm, living, breathing, utterly believable family that readers come to care about desperately. And through her characters' eyes, she presents the whole terrible conflict of the war, so that readers will feel that they have actually experienced it.

In any good historical novel, the history is an integral part of the story, not just a background. Characters should be caught up in events that affect their lives. The actual event—the landing at Plymouth Rock, the battle at Gettysburg, the wagon trains opening up the West—may be familiar, but if the characters are people that readers relate to, laugh with, cry with, worry with, tremble with, then these facts of history take on a new dimension.

Another writer who totally captures the era she writes about is Jill Paton Walsh. In *Grace* (Farrar, 1992), she undertakes an even riskier task, because Grace Darling was a real person.

Walsh has kept her narrative as true to life as possible, working from letters, journals, and newspaper articles. (Grace became a national heroine when she assisted her father, a lighthouse keeper, in rescuing survivors of a tragic shipwreck.) The author admits, however, to having imagined certain events and conversations. Nonetheless, and with admirable discipline, she keeps Grace's speech, thoughts, and behavior strictly within her own time. The novel is told in the first person, and it is Grace's voice throughout. One would be hard put to tell where facts end and imagination begins.

Also, although the deluge of publicity that followed this rescue was largely due to the fact that a mere girl had temporarily taken over a man's job, Walsh never turns her story into a feminist tract. In 19th-century England, as in America, there was a sharp division of labor among the sexes, and while Grace could stand her watch and tend the lamps in the lighthouse, she was also expected to cook, scrub, polish, mend, and sew. And these things she regarded as her duty.

Neither of these books talks down to readers. In both of them, the characters speak in the local dialect and write in the manner of the day. This can present a challenge to present-day youngsters reared on television dialogue, but readers worth their salt will soon discover the rich rhythms and poetry in the 19th-century speech that make the extra effort well worthwhile.

Another book that rings true is Gloria Skurzynski's *Good-bye, Billy Radish* (Bradbury, 1992). Although somewhat episodic at first, it builds to a powerful and moving conclusion, and at the same time creates a clear and fully realized picture of life in a harsh steel-mill town during the First World War.

Young Hank and the older, more mature Billy are firmly rooted in their own time. Their pleasures include a Fourth of July parade, going on rides at a carnival, and a growing awareness of girls. Within this simple coming-of-age story, Skurzynski gives readers a glimpse into the terrifying conditions of the mills, the struggles of immigrant families to become part of America, the growing understanding of the actual horrors of that far away war, and the cruel reality of the influenza epidemic at home. She has taken an era and made it come alive.

This is what historical novels are all about. They give children a chance to know what it was like to grow up without all the trappings of modern life, as well as an understanding of the struggles and courage of their parents, grandparents, and great-grandparents. They give them a sense of their roots. They also point up some of the terrible things that were done, often in ignorance, in the name of progress.

Good historical fiction is more than a dry history lesson; it re-creates the past, not just events, but the common thread of humanity that unites us with those events. As in all good fiction, it shows us life, filtered through the imagination. ▲

ANNOTATED JOURNAL ARTICLES

Bruner, Katharine Everett. "Stereotypes in Juvenile Historical Fiction," *School Library Journal* (September 1988): 124-25.

The author points out specific examples of stereotyped characters in well-known historical fiction novels for children and young adults. The story can take a dangerous twist when the prejudiced character becomes the authoritative narrator.

Caywood, Carolyn. "Rome Through Historical Fiction," *School Library Journal* (September 1994): 152.

The author draws parallels between our times and those of ancient Rome, citing many historical novels as examples. The ancient Romans' struggle with the transition from republic to empire, the imposition of a single culture across the known world, and the need to maintain peace and order among diverse peoples seems like a rehearsal for the present century.

Chauvette, Cathy. "Journeys into the Past: The Power of Historical Fiction," *School Library Journal* (June 1992): 51-52.

It is difficult to write historical fiction, because there are so many constraints. There are "docunovels," which take the basic facts and then develop a story suitable for a television documentary, with lots of extras to make the story more dramatic. There are also "Jewett" novels where everyday survival is the main concern. The term *Jewett* refers to Sarah Orne Jewett (1849-1909) who wrote about the lonely lives of isolated people in rural Maine. Laura Ingalls Wilder stories are good examples of Jewett novels.

ANNOTATED BIBLIOGRAPHY

Beatty, Patricia. *Jayhawker.* Morrow Junior Books, 1992.

A jayhawker was a Kansas abolitionist who actively tried to end slavery during the Civil War era. Lije accompanied his father and cousins across the border to Missouri to raid farms or pick up runaway slaves along the river. When Lije's father is killed by slavers during a raid, Lije decides to serve as a spy for the Union. This is no easy task, as the Confederate band of which Lije is now a part includes ruthless Charley Quantrill, sharpshooter Jim Hickok, and young, sullen Jesse James.

Drucker, Malka, and Michael Halperin. *Jacob's Rescue: A Holocaust Story.* Bantam Skylark, 1993.

This is the true story of Alex and Mela Roslan and their rescue of Jacob and David Gutgeld. Alex and Mela lived in Warsaw, Poland, and they saved Jacob from the Warsaw ghetto in 1941. David, his younger brother, who passed as a Gentile, was brought to them later. The brothers hid with the Roslans and their family until the Germans retreated from Poland in defeat. The Roslans risked their lives to save the Jewish children. In 1981, Mela and Alex received the Righteous Among the Nations award from the Israeli government. Israel gives this award to non-Jews who risked their lives to save Jews during the Holocaust. The book ends with a statement that can be applied to all times and all people: "Perhaps only a few people can be as selfless and courageous as the Roslans, but everyone can pay attention to another's suffering and try to help."

Hansen, Joyce. *The Captive.* Scholastic Paper, 1994.

Oppong, a slave, was treated like a member of the family. He warns Kofi's father of impending danger at the yearly royal celebration. Kwame, the father, leaves with his two elder sons and bodyguards. Kofi, 12 years of age, decides to follow, and instead of a day of celebration he witnesses the deceit of Oppong. Kofi is captured and taken aboard a slaver bound for the New World and new adventures.

Hesse, Karen. *Letters from Rifka.* Henry Holt, 1992.

Rifka records the events of her journey to America in a volume of poetry by Alexander Pushkin, a gift from her cousin, Toval, whom she left behind in Russia. The many hardships that Rifka and her family endure give the reader a powerful insight into the horrors of the world for Jews in 1919.

Kudlinski, Kathleen V. *Pearl Harbor Is Burning!* Viking, 1991.

Kenji befriends Frank, a new boy in the local Hawaiian fifth grade. On December 7, Frank hurries to meet Kenji at his tree fort. The best part of the tree fort is its view of Pearl Harbor and the whole Pacific Fleet. A buzzing sound fills the sky, but the boys don't even bother to look up, assuming that it is another practice raid. Soon, though, the boys realize that a Japanese plane is heading right for them.

Polacco, Patricia. *Pink and Say.* Philomel, 1994.

This story was passed from great-grandfather to grandmother, to son and then to daughter, Patricia Polacco. Sheldon Curtis, a young Union boy from Ohio, lay wounded in a pasture in Georgia. Pinkus Aylee found Sheldon after Pinkus was separated from the 48th colored company. Pinkus, mindful of marauding Confederate troops, carried Say (Sheldon) to his mother, sweet Moe Moe Bay. They stayed there while Say recovered, until the marauders rode in, tragically killing Moe Moe and ultimately Pink. Say, who survived Andersonville, passed the story on.

BIBLIOGRAPHY

Anderson, Joan. *The First Thanksgiving Feast.* Clarion Books, 1983.

Armstrong, William H. *Sounder.* Harper & Row, 1969.

Avi. *The Fighting Ground.* J. B. Lippincott, 1984.

———. *The True Confessions of Charlotte Doyle.* Orchard, 1990.

Beatty, Patricia. *Be Ever Hopeful, Hannalee.* Morrow Junior Books, 1988.

———. *Charley Skedaddle.* Morrow Junior Books, 1988.

———. *Jayhawker.* Morrow Junior Books, 1991.

Brenner, Barbara. *Wagon Wheels.* Harper & Row, 1993.

Brink, Carol Ryrie. *Caddie Woodlawn.* Macmillan, 1973.

Bulla, Clyde Robert. *A Lion to Guard Us.* Scholastic, 1981.

Carter, Dorothy Sharp. *His Majesty, Queen Hatshepsut.* J. B. Lippincott, 1987.

Choi, Sook Nyul. *Year of Impossible Goodbyes.* Houghton Mifflin, 1991.

Cohen, Barbara. *Molly's Pilgrim.* Lothrop, Lee & Shepard, 1983.

Collier, James Lincoln, and Christopher Collier. *The Bloody Country.* Four Winds Press, 1976.

———. *Jump Ship to Freedom.* Delacorte Press, 1981.

Conrad, Pam. *Pedro's Journal.* Caroline House, 1991.

———. *Prairie Songs.* Harper & Row, 1985.

Crew, Linda. *Children of the River.* Delacorte Press, 1989.

Dalgliesh, Alice. *The Courage of Sarah Noble.* Charles Scribner's Sons, 1954.

De Angeli, Marguerite. *The Door in the Wall.* Doubleday, 1949.

Dorris, Michael. *Morning Girl*. Little, Brown, 1992.

Edmonds, Walter D. *The Matchlock Gun*. Dodd, Mead, 1941.

Fleischman, Paul. *The Borning Room*. HarperCollins, 1991.

Forbes, Esther. *Johnny Tremain*. Houghton Mifflin, 1946.

Fox, Paula. *Slave Dancer*. Bradbury Press, 1973.

Fritz, Jean. *Cabin Faced West*. Coward-McCann, 1958.

———. *George Washington's Breakfast*. Coward-McCann, 1969.

Gordon, Sheila. *Waiting for the Rain*. Orchard, 1987.

Greene, Bette. *The Summer of My German Soldier*. Bantam Books, 1984.

Hamilton, Virginia. *Anthony Burns: The Defeat and Triumph of a Fugitive Slave*. Alfred A. Knopf, 1988.

Harvey, Brett. *Immigrant Girl: Becky of Eldridge Street*. Holiday House, 1987.

Hesse, Karen. *Letters from Rifka*. Henry Holt, 1992.

Hooks, William H. *Pioneer Cat*. Random House, 1988.

Keith, Harold. *Rifles for Watie*. Thomas Y. Crowell, 1957.

Konigsburg, E. L. *A Proud Taste for Scarlet and Miniver*. Atheneum, 1973.

Korman, Justin. *Davy Crockett at the Alamo*. Disney Press, 1991.

Lasky, Kathryn. *The Night Journey*. Puffin Paper, 1986.

Lenski, Lois. *Strawberry Girl*. Dell Yearling, 1945.

Levitin, Sonia. *Journey to America*. Atheneum, 1970.

———. *The Return*. Atheneum, 1987.

Lord, Betty Bao. *In the Year of the Boar and Jackie Robinson*. HarperCollins, 1984.

Lowry, Lois. *Number the Stars*. Houghton Mifflin, 1989.

MacLachlan, Patricia. *Sarah, Plain and Tall*. HarperCollins, 1989.

———. *Three Names*. HarperCollins, 1991.

McSwigan, Marie. *Snow Treasure*. Scholastic, 1986.

Moeri, Louise. *Save Queen of Sheba*. E. P. Dutton, 1981.

Nixon, Joan Lowry. *A Family Apart*. Bantam Books, 1987.

O'Dell, Scott. *Island of the Blue Dolphins*. Houghton Mifflin, 1960.

———. *Sarah Bishop*. Houghton Mifflin, 1980.

———. *Sing Down the Moon*. Houghton Mifflin, 1970.

O'Neal, Zibby. *A Long Way to Go*. Viking, 1990.

Orlev, Uri. *The Island on Bird Street*. Houghton Mifflin, 1984.

———. *The Man from the Other Side*. Houghton Mifflin, 1991.

Paterson, Katherine. *Lyddie*. Lodestar, 1991.

———. *The Master Puppeteer*. Harper & Row, 1976.

———. *Rebels of the Heavenly Kingdom*. Lodestar, 1983.

Petry, Ann. *Tituba of Salem Village*. Thomas Y. Crowell, 1964.

Reeder, Carolyn. *Shades of Gray*. Macmillan, 1989.

Reiss, Johanna. *The Upstairs Room*. Thomas Y. Crowell, 1972.

Sewall, Marcia. *The Pilgrims of Plimoth*. Atheneum, 1986.

Skurzynski, Gloria. *Good-bye, Billy Radish*. Bradbury Press, 1992.

Speare, Elizabeth. *The Sign of the Beaver*. Houghton Mifflin, 1983.

———. *The Witch of Blackbird Pond*. Houghton Mifflin, 1958.

Sutcliff, Rosemary. *Flame-Colored Taffeta*. Farrar, Straus & Giroux, 1986.

———. *Frontier Wolf*. Oxford University Press, 1980.

Taylor, Mildred D. *Let the Circle Be Unbroken*. Bantam Books, 1983.

———. *Roll of Thunder, Hear My Cry*. Bantam Books, 1976.

Turner, Ann. *Dakota Dugout*. Macmillan, 1985.

———. *Katie's Trunk*. Macmillan, 1992.

Walsh, Paton. *Grace*. Farrar, Straus & Giroux, 1992.

Waters, Kate. *Sarah Morton's Day: A Day in the Life of a Pilgrim Girl*. Scholastic, 1989.

Wilder, Laura Ingalls. *Little House in the Big Woods*. Harper & Row, 1953.

Wisler, G. Clifton. *Red Cap*. Lodestar, 1991.

Yep, Laurence. *The Rainbow People*. HarperCollins, 1989.

Yolen, Jane. *The Devil's Arithmetic*. Viking Kestrel, 1988.

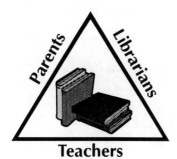

Parents · Librarians · Teachers

Chapter 5

Picture Books for Young and Old

OVERVIEW

Picture books can range from board books, illustrated songs, nursery rhymes, alphabet books, and counting books for babies or toddlers to ethnic tales, folklore, and contemporary short fantasies. Now, more than ever before, sophisticated picture books—as works of art and social commentary—are reaching upper elementary, middle, and even high school readers.

Picture books offer the opportunity to sit, look, and enjoy. Old and young alike smile in response to funny pictures and concentrate on really beautiful pictures. Picture books can move as quickly as an action-packed novel, with lots of potential for reading aloud. They can also be a cross between a painting and poetry, to be enjoyed at leisure. Good picture books keep the attention of children and make them want more good picture books!

GUIDED READING QUESTIONS

1. Compare and contrast the styles and art forms of your books.

2. Are the illustrations consistent with and appropriate to the storyline?

3. Does the author avoid stereotypes of race and gender?

4. Do the illustrations reflect the theme of the book? If so, how?

5. What technique is used to convey feelings or moods? Was it successful?

6. Is anything unusual about the format or layout of the book?

7. Are the illustrations and storylines complementary, or does one element dominate the other?

8. Are the books appropriate for both young and old readers? If not, what age group would you recommend?

9. If you have a favorite picture book of your own at home, please bring it to share.

From *The Reading Connection*. © 1997. Libraries Unlimited. (800) 237-6124.

JOURNAL ARTICLE

The Picture Book Problem

An "expensive crumb" means memorable pictures
with forgettable stories.

There have always been more picture books published each year than the library market needs or than booksellers can sell. It's a chronic selection problem that has taken a turn for the worse in this year of our celebration of the 50th anniversary of the award of the Caldecott Medal, established to promote the very best in illustrated books for children.

The reason behind the rise in the numbers of picture books is not hard to guess. Like every other business that is affected by the birth rate, the publishers of books for children have heard or read the siren songs of the demographers. For the last five years, these dabblers in population projections have forecast a rise in the number of births each year in the United States.

However, down in the fine print below the headlines, the forecasters are usually careful to note that the rise in the birth rate can be traced to unabating or increasing numbers of babies produced by racial and ethnic minorities as well as by unwed, teenaged girls. And, there you have one of the most glaring failures of the historic and current oversupply of picture books— the near absence of black, brown, red or yellow faces—even in crowd scenes.

This is a real, longstanding problem. It becomes more problematic when you match the origins of the baby boomlet against the pervasive concerns shared by educators and the general society: the crying need to introduce and to nurture, from the earliest ages, an appetite for reading. Population minority groups on their way to becoming majorities in some areas need picture books with which both children and their parents can identify. Too few of this sort are being published today and too few live on the publishers' backlists.

There are other selection problems presented by the growing number of picture books aimed at the diminishing number of white, middle-class children. Two problems that stand out are the problem of expense and the problem of literary standards. *SLJ* Book Review so seldom finds a new picture book priced under the $12 to $15 range that when a 32-page picture book turns up with a lower price tag it becomes a matter of corridor comment. That's got to be a problem for children's departments in public libraries and in elementary school libraries. In the case of the schools, we know that the median per pupil book expenditure of $4.45 buys less than a third to a quarter of one new picture book.

By Lillian N. Gerhardt. Reprinted with permission from *School Library Journal* (September 1987), page 94. Lillian Gerhardt is editor-in-chief of *School Library Journal.*

Among those who care deeply for children and their books, the real *ouch!* comes in recognizing how many new picture books are brought into existence merely as shaky showcases for illustrators. We see so many new picture books with good-to-great talent in the art department and so few with storylines worth five minutes of any parent's or child's time. These titles are expensively weak investments in the effort to create life-long readers.

We've coined a critical shorthand term in *SLJ*'s office to describe such picture books—"expensive crumbs." The most expensive of these crumbs have always been, and continue to be, those picture books for which the texts are drawn from folklore or original stories now in the public domain. The author thus requires no royalty but the unit price stays high. How many picture books separate from story collections do you need in a library collection? Apparently, the children's book publishers have always been and are still willing to issue more than the library market can bear.

Spare a kindly thought for the booksellers who are rising to the wave of concern for the inoculation of young children with a love of reading. Picture books at $15 a pop are a hard sell for bookstores which need satisfied adult customers. Notice, the next time you're in a bookstore specializing in books for children, how heavily these booksellers depend on older titles among the picture books—those first discovered, tested, purchased, and endlessly replaced by librarians. That's good for them. It's even better for us, when you stop to think about it.

The library answer to the outpouring of high-priced, eye-catching, but mind-losing new picture books is simple; relentlessly high selection standards that demand strong characters and strong stories supported by strong illustrations. ▲

ANNOTATED JOURNAL ARTICLES

Evans, Dilys. "An Extraordinary Vision: Picture Books of the Nineties," *Horn Book Magazine* (November-December 1992): 759-63.

Picture books in the 1990s demonstrate that children are more sophisticated visually and verbally. Bright, bold colors, along with the use of innovative materials, allow many new forms of expression. Lane Smith, David Wisniewski, and Jeannie Baker are some of the illustrators discussed in this article.

Goldenberg, Carol. "The Design and Typography of Children's Books," *Horn Book Magazine* (September-October 1993): 559-67.

All books are designed. The better the design and typography of the book, the less that fact is apparent to the reader. The processes of book design and production are explained. In the future, books will still have to be designed, no matter what form they take.

Krauthammer, Charles. "Hiroshima, Mon Petit," *Time* (March 27, 1995): 80.

Social realism is invading the rosy world of the seven-year-old. Why are we exposing children to dishonest and disturbing books such as *Smoky Night* and *Let the Celebrations Begin*? These types of books pervert the innocence of children. A rebuttal commentary on this thought-provoking essay can be found in *School Library Journal* (May 1995): 10-11.

Rovenger, Judith. "Picture Books for Older Children," *School Library Journal* (May 1987): 38-39.

Picture books should be shared with as wide an audience as possible. Several titles are discussed, including *The Mysteries of Harris Burdick*, *Piggybook*, and *Hey, Al*. Picture books can be "little jewels of literature."

Silvey, Anita. "Sunspots," *Horn Book Magazine* (May-June 1993): 260.

For a while, picture books were caught up in the new technology of printing. Bold colors and various artistic media dominated the field. Now it appears that quality stories, technology, and art are being combined to produce picture books that will be read again and again.

ANNOTATED BIBLIOGRAPHY

Cherry, Lynne. *The Armadillo from Amarillo*. Illustrated by Lynne Cherry. Harcourt Brace Jovanovich, 1994.

Sasparillo, an armadillo from Texas, wondered, "Where in the world am I?" From the postcards and full-page illustrations, we follow him north through Texas. He meets an eagle and hops on the bird's back. They fly higher and higher until Sasparillo finds the answer to his question.

Isaacs, Anne. *Swamp Angel*. Illustrated by Paul O. Zelinsky. Dutton Children's Books, 1994.

A tall tale about Angelica Longrider, the greatest woodswoman in Tennessee, also known as Swamp Angel. She joined a competition to catch the huge bear, Thundering Tarnation. When the two fought, they stirred up so much dust that those hills are still called the Smoky Mountains. Angelica and Thundering Tarnation were so exhausted that they both fell asleep. Angelica snored down a tree, which killed the bear; she responded, "Confound it, varmint, if you warn't the most wondrous heap of trouble I ever come to grips with!"

Johnson, Angela. *Julius*. Illustrated by Dav Pilkey. Orchard, 1993.

Maya's grandfather lived part of the time in Alaska. On one of his visits home, he brings Maya a pig to teach her fun and sharing. Maya loves Julius immediately, and she shares what she learns from Julius with her friends. One can't help but love Julius.

Ludwig, Warren. *Good Morning, Granny Rose.* Illustrated by Warren Ludwig. Putnam, 1990.

Granny Rose and her dog Henry go to watch the sunrise at Lookout Ridge. On their return, they walk smack-dab into a blizzard. Henry finds a cave for protection against the storm. They soon fall asleep and are awakened by a grunt and a snort nearby. This Arkansas folktale ends in a unique way that children enjoy.

Polacco, Patricia. *Thundercake.* Illustrated by Patricia Polacco. Philomel, 1990.

Thundercake will take any child's mind off an approaching storm. The grandchild in the story is afraid of storms until Grandma gets her to come out from under the bed. Together they gather all the necessary ingredients to make thundercake. By the time they have made the cake, the little girl realizes that she is brave and that brave people are not afraid of sounds. The recipe is included.

Sis, Peter. *Komodo.* Illustrated by Peter Sis. Greenwillow Books, 1993.

A short tale about a boy who loves dragons. His parents take him to the Indonesian island of Komodo. At first the boy is disappointed when he lands on the island, but after an encounter with a dragon he thinks it's the best place he has ever been.

Steig, William. *Brave Irene.* Illustrated by William Steig. Farrar, Straus & Giroux, 1986.

Irene Bobbin, a dressmaker's daughter, offers to deliver a ball gown to the duchess for her sick mother. As Irene plows through snow, fierce winds wrestle the dress away from her. Irene decides to trudge on and explain the mishap in person. She is cold, lost, and miserable, but finally uses the empty box as a sled to reach the glittering palace. To her amazement, she finds the ball gown pressed against the trunk of a tree, held there by the wind. Due to bad weather, Irene spends the night and even dances at the ball. What adventures she will have to share with her mother!

Stevens, Janet. *Tops and Bottoms.* Illustrated by Janet Stevens. Harcourt Brace Jovanovich, 1995.

Bear has lots of land but is lazy. All Bear wants to do is sleep. Hare lives down the road and sells his land to Bear to pay off a debt. Hare outwits Bear by proposing a partnership: Hare will work Bear's land and they will split the harvest. All Bear has to do is choose which half he wants, top or bottom. The format and illustrations match this tale, which has roots in the slave stories of the American South.

Wood, Audrey. *Heckedy Peg.* Illustrated by Don Wood. Harcourt Brace Jovanovich, 1987.

Heckedy Peg is based on a 16th-century children's game that is still played today. Seven children, named after the days of the week, are transformed by a witch into food. Their mother saves them by guessing which food is which child. She knows who they are by the foods they like, and thus she breaks the witch's spell.

BIBLIOGRAPHY

Alcorn, Johnny. *Rembrandt's Beret.* Illustrated by Stephen Alcorn. Tambourine, 1991.

Bartone, Elisa. *Peppe the Lamplighter.* Illustrated by Ted Lewin. Lothrop, Lee & Shepard, 1993.

Bedard, Michael. *Emily.* Illustrated by Barbara Cooney. Doubleday, 1992.

Blanc, Esther. *Berchick.* Illustrated by Tennessee Dixon. Volcano, 1989.

Bunting, Eve. *The Day Before Christmas.* Illustrated by Beth Peck. Clarion Books, 1992.

———. *Fly Away Home.* Illustrated by Ronald Himler. Clarion Books, 1991.

———. *How Many Days to America.* Illustrated by Beth Peck. Houghton Mifflin, 1988.

———. *The Wall.* Illustrated by Ronald Himler. Clarion Books, 1990.

Cherry, Lynne. *The Great Kapok Tree.* Illustrated by Lynne Cherry. Harcourt Brace Jovanovich, 1992.

———. *A River Ran Wild.* Illustrated by Lynne Cherry. Harcourt Brace Jovanovich, 1992.

Cooney, Barbara. *Miss Rumphius.* Illustrated by Barbara Cooney. Viking, 1982.

dePaola, Tomie. *Nana Upstairs & Nana Downstairs.* Illustrated by Tomie dePaola. Puffin Books, 1973.

———. *Now One Foot, Now the Other.* Illustrated by Tomie dePaola. Putnam, 1981.

———. *Tom.* Illustrated by Tomie dePaola. Putnam, 1993.

Garland, Sherry. *The Lotus Seed.* Illustrated by Tatsuro Kluchi. Harcourt Brace Jovanovich, 1993.

Harvey, Brett. *Cassie's Journey: Going West in the 1860's.* Illustrated by Deborah Kogan Ray. Holiday House, 1988.

———. *Immigrant Girl: Becky of Eldridge Street.* Illustrated by Deborah Kogan Ray. Holiday House, 1987.

Heide, Florence Parry, and Judith Heide Gilliland. *Sami and the Time of the Troubles.* Illustrated by Ted Lewin. Clarion Books, 1992.

Hest, Amy. *The Mommy Exchange.* Illustrated by DyAnne DiSalvo-Ryan. Four Winds Press, 1988.

Hoyt-Goldsmith, Diane. *Arctic Hunter.* Illustrated by Lawrence Migdale. Holiday House, 1992.

———. *Pueblo Storyteller.* Illustrated by Lawrence Migdale. Holiday House, 1991.

Innocenti, Roberto, and Christophe Gallaz. *Rose Blanche.* Illustrated by Roberto Innocenti. Creative Education, 1986.

Jonas, Ann. *The 13th Clue.* Illustrated by Ann Jonas. Greenwillow Books, 1992.

Joyce, William. *A Day with Wilbur Robinson.* Illustrated by William Joyce. Harper & Row, 1990.

Leighton, Maxinne Rhea. *An Ellis Island Christmas.* Illustrated by Dennis Nolan. Harper & Row, 1990.

Levitin, Sonia. *The Man Who Kept His Heart in a Bucket.* Illustrated by Jerry Pinkney. Dial Books for Young Readers, 1991.

Lionni, Leo. *Swimmy.* Illustrated by Leo Lionni. Pantheon, 1963.

MacLachlan, Patricia. *Three Names.* Illustrated by Alexander Pertzoff. HarperCollins, 1991.

Martin, Bill, and John Archambault. *Knots on a Counting Rope.* Illustrated by Ted Lewin. Henry Holt, 1987.

Medearis, Angela Shelf. *Dancing with the Indians.* Illustrated by Samuel Byrd. Holiday House, 1991.

Melmed, Laura Krauss. *The First Song Ever Sung.* Illustrated by Ed Young. Lothrop, Lee & Shepard, 1993.

Mills, Lauren. *The Rag Coat.* Illustrated by Lauren Mills. Little, Brown, 1991.

Mollel, Tololwa M. *The Orphan Boy.* Illustrated by Paul Morin. Houghton Mifflin, 1991.

Olson, Arielle North. *The Lighthouse Keeper's Daughter.* Illustrated by Elaine Wentworth. Little, Brown, 1987.

Paterson, Katherine. *The King's Equal.* Illustrated by Vladimir Vagin. HarperCollins, 1992.

———. *The Tale of the Mandarin Ducks.* Illustrated by Leo Dillon and Diane Dillon. E. P. Dutton, 1992.

Perrault, Charles. *Puss in Boots*. Illustrated by Fred Marcellino. Farrar, Straus & Giroux, 1990.

Polacco, Patricia. *The Bee Tree*. Illustrated by Patricia Polacco. Philomel, 1993.

———. *The Keeping Quilt*. Illustrated by Patricia Polacco. Simon & Schuster, 1988.

———. *Rechenka's Eggs*. Illustrated by Patricia Polacco. Philomel, 1988.

Ringgold, Faith. *Aunt Harriet's Underground Railroad in the Sky*. Illustrated by Faith Ringgold. Crown, 1992.

———. *Tar Beach*. Illustrated by Faith Ringgold. Crown, 1991.

Say, Allen. *Grandfather's Journey*. Illustrated by Allen Say. Houghton Mifflin, 1993.

———. *River Dream*. Illustrated by Allen Say. Houghton Mifflin, 1988.

———. *Tree of Cranes*. Illustrated by Allen Say. Houghton Mifflin, 1991.

Schoenherr, John. *Bear*. Illustrated by John Schoenherr. Philomel, 1991.

Scieszka, Jon. *The Stinky Cheese Man and Other Fairly Stupid Tales*. Illustrated by Lane Smith. Viking, 1992.

———. *The True Story of the 3 Little Pigs by A. Wolf*. Illustrated by Lane Smith. Viking, 1989.

Seuss, Dr. *The Butter Battle Book*. Illustrated by Dr. Seuss. Random House, 1984.

———. *Oh, the Places You'll Go*. Illustrated by Dr. Seuss. Random House, 1990.

Siebert, Diane. *Sierra*. Illustrated by Wendell Minor. HarperCollins, 1991.

Sis, Peter. *A Small Tall Tale*. Illustrated by Peter Sis. Alfred A. Knopf, 1993.

Snyder, Diane. *The Boy of the Three Year Nap*. Illustrated by Allen Say. Houghton Mifflin, 1988.

Steig, William. *Doctor De Soto*. Illustrated by William Steig. Farrar, Straus & Giroux, 1982.

Steptoe, John. *The Story of Jumping Mouse*. Illustrated by John Steptoe. Lothrop, Lee & Shepard, 1984.

Sutcliff, Rosemary. *The Minstrel and the Dragon Pup*. Illustrated by Emma C. Clark. Candlewick Press, 1993.

Tejima, Keizaburo. *Fox's Dream*. Illustrated by Keizaburo Tejima. Philomel, 1987.

Van Allsburg, Chris. *The Mysteries of Harris Burdick*. Illustrated by Chris Van Allsburg. Houghton Mifflin, 1984.

———. *The Polar Express*. Illustrated by Chris Van Allsburg. Houghton Mifflin, 1985.

———. *The Widow's Broom*. Illustrated by Chris Van Allsburg. Houghton Mifflin, 1985.

———. *The Wretched Stone*. Illustrated by Chris Van Allsburg. Houghton Mifflin, 1991.

———. *The Z Was Zapped: A Play in Twenty-Six Acts*. Illustrated by Chris Van Allsburg. Houghton Mifflin, 1987.

Wild, Margaret. *Let the Celebrations Begin!* Illustrated by Julie Vivas. Orchard, 1991.

Wisniewski, David. *Sundiata: Lion King of Mali*. Illustrated by David Wisniewski. Houghton Mifflin, 1992.

Yolen, Jane. *Wings*. Illustrated by Dennis Nolan. Harcourt Brace Jovanovich, 1991.

Ziefert, Harriet. *A New Coat for Anna*. Illustrated by Anita Lobel. Alfred A. Knopf, 1986.

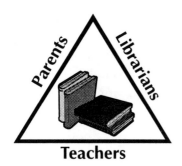

Chapter 6

Multicultural Literature

OVERVIEW

Children's literature has characterized people of diverse cultures in a trite manner for a long time. Mostly, these portrayals have been erroneous and insensitive. For too many years, black Americans were neither mentioned nor pictured in children's literature. Multicultural literature first appeared during the late 1970s, and the genre has been increasing in popularity since then. This has helped teachers who see increasing cultural diversity in the classroom. These books break through old, hackneyed assumptions regarding people from different cultures and help students to better understand the struggles, feelings, and emotions of other ethnic groups.

As parents and educators, we strive to make our students cognizant and accepting of cultural diversity. We should emphasize similarities and provide a better understanding and, we hope, a greater tolerance of others through good multicultural literature.

GUIDED READING QUESTIONS

1. Does your book fit the definition of multicultural literature?

2. Is it a good representation?

3. Are there stereotypes?

4. Does the book broaden your understanding of the culture, or does it describe things you already knew?

5. Should your book be included in a bibliography of quality multicultural books?

Making Connections: Introducing Multicultural Books

Stories affect us in much the same way that exposure to any other art form does.

With the recent emphasis on multiculturalism and the interest in multicultural literature, school and public librarians may wonder what implications these issues have on serving patrons in their individual libraries. Coping with an already full platter, they may feel overwhelmed at the thought of fitting yet another item onto the agenda. Yet connecting books with children is second nature to them and making multicultural books part of the library experience should be neither difficult nor novel. My discussion here will briefly mention the various types of multicultural books, a few of the ways in which they can be used with children, and highlight some authors who have succeeded in making connections through their work.

Books about children from other cultures are sitting all over our library shelves. There are titles translated from other languages into English, or those originally written in English but set in other countries; some convey a very strong sense of another culture, yet also express commonly felt emotions. There are still others in which setting seems incidental, yet the themes and characters have universal appeal. Finally, there are stories about children who have been transplanted from other cultures to this country, which tell how they have adapted to their new lives. There are novels, picture books, folktales, and works of nonfiction. There is no dearth of material.

What about our readers? Who are they? Many of us live in communities that have tremendous ethnic and cultural diversity. A quick look at the list of children's foreign language books available from the central collection at the Hempstead Public Library in Nassau County, New York, reveals languages from Arabic to Punjabi, from Hebrew to Farsi, from Cambodian-Khmer to Ukrainian. Our library collections can and should reflect this cultural diversity even if our own communities do not.

A recent newspaper article reported that local increases in population were due predominantly to growth in the Hispanic community. Yet, for younger readers, there has been very little published to date about this group or the diverse cultures that make up the Spanish-speaking community (Puerto Ricans, Mexicans, Central and South Americans). There are, however, a few noteworthy examples. Children's Book Press is a small press that publishes stories from minority and new immigrant cultures in America today. *Uncle Nacho's Hat* (Children's Book Pr., 1989), adapted from a Nicaraguan folktale by Harriet Rohmer, uses a bilingual text and bright

By Corinne Camarata. Reprinted with permission from *School Library Journal* (September 1991), page 190. Corinne Camarata is Director of Children's Services, Port Washington Public Library, NY.

folk-art style illustrations in primary colors to tell the gently humorous story of Uncle Nacho's obsession with his old hat and how he is finally persuaded that change can be a good thing.

While they are not immigrants, Native-American peoples have had to adapt to an alien culture, and today their children straddle two societies. Marcia Keegan's *Pueblo Boy* (Cobblehill: Dutton, 1991) is a photo-documentary of ten-year-old Timmy Roybal, who lives with his family at the San Ildefonso Pueblo in New Mexico. Full-color photos capture the dramatic natural surroundings and introduce readers to the details of the boy's life. His Pueblo home is a modern middle-class dwelling adorned with the art and handiwork of his relatives. Roman Catholic and ancient Pueblo customs coexist here and while Timmy uses computers and prepares for the future, he is equally concerned about learning the songs, dances, and rituals of his clan that have been passed down for 10,000 years.

Not only do such titles help to acquaint children with the background and traditions of their friends and classmates, humanizing what may be strange or different; they also act as a sort of mirror for newly immigrated children, something in which to find a little of their own image, a connection to a new society that is now their own.

There are major gaps in other areas as well. For example, there are almost no stories about the Arab culture for younger readers. *The Day of Ahmed's Secret* (Lothrop, 1990) by Florence Heide & Judith Heide Gilliland is a notable one. Ted Lewin's glowing paintings depict a young boy's native Cairo as he goes about his daily work anxious for the day to end so that he can reveal his secret to his family; he has learned to write his name. The exotic locale only underscores the universality of this life experience.

Librarians have various ways of connecting a book with a child. Aside from the direct one-on-one approach of recommending—convincing a particular child to take out a particular book and hopefully read it—we have opportunities to introduce children to multicultural books in story hours (that staple of children's library programming), in book discussion groups, by developing reading lists, and now, hopefully, through our involvement in developing curriculum for whole language reading and social studies programs in the schools.

Folktales have long been a popular way to introduce other cultures to our children. The stories are short, accessible, and entertaining, running the gamut of human emotion and experience. Common threads often run through stories from different countries, with each culture adapting or embellishing, and then incorporating its unique idiosyncrasies into the tale. A wide range of folktale collections are available, as well as many single stories that are published in picture-book format. There is a wealth of material to draw from in this genre, and new retellings appear all the time.

Children's novels set in other countries are most likely to be found in translation from the original language, although there are successful historical novels, written by American authors, that have foreign settings. Lois Lowry's Newbery Award winning story, *Number the Stars* (Houghton), about two young friends caught up in Denmark's struggle to save its Jewish citizens during World War II; and Billi Rosen's *Andi's War* (Dutton, both 1989), about a family torn apart and trying to survive during the Greek civil war, are two fine examples.

Usually more surefire in popularity are books set in the United States, such as Laurence Yep's *Dragonwings* (Harper-Collins, 1975), a wonderful tale of the clash of cultures, as a young Chinese boy adjusts to life in turn-of-the-century San Francisco. There is also Yoshika Uchida's *Journey to Topaz* (Creative Arts Bk., 1985) which describes the experiences of 11-year-old Yuki and her family, victims of Executive Order 9066, who are sent to a Japanese internment camp.

In any case, stories with child appeal are often taken from personal background, childhood experience, or family history. They can be fictionalized, as was Jean Fritz's account of her childhood in China, *Homesick* (Putnam, 1982); or published as nonfiction, like Esther Hautzig's *Endless Steppe* (HarperCollins, 1968), which recounts the years she and her family spent in Siberia during World War II, having been branded capitalist enemies of the people by the Russians who occupied northeastern Poland in 1941. Fascinating details, a far-away setting, a child's perspective, and good storytelling are what make these titles so engaging.

As with writers of fiction and nonfiction, authors who are successful in the picture-book format often draw on personal experience or contacts with individuals from other cultures. In these books setting is important, and is depicted not only through the text, but in the illustrations, which are an integral part of the story.

My Uncle Nikos (HarperCollins, 1982; o.p.), by Julie Delton, takes place in a little village in the mountains of Greece, where the older men wear straw hats and drink ouzo. Dinner is cooked outside in a cooking pit piled with dry cypress branches. But regardless of its trappings, this is a simple intergenerational story about a little girl and her older uncle taking pleasure in each other's company, enjoying routines both simple and rustic.

Often a story revolves around a situation or event unique to the culture portrayed. Such is the case with Jan Andrews's *The Very Last First Time* (McElderry, 1986). A young Inuit girl and her mother go to gather mussels from the bottom of the sea at low tide. After cutting a hole in the ice, Eva is lowered to the ocean floor, using lighted candles to find her way. At one point Eva fears she may not find her way back. The excitement and strangeness, and the sense of adventure and accomplishment combine to make this a compelling and appealing work.

Another picture book that is specific to a time and place yet transcends both is *Tar Beach* (Crown, 1991), written and illustrated by Faith Ringgold. Fantasy and social history blend in this story of a black child living in New York City in the 1930s. Lavish folk-art paintings in velvety jewel tones dominate the pages of this book that was originally designed as a quilt. Cassie Lightfoot, eight years old, imagines she can fly above the tiny rooftop of her family's apartment building, the tar beach of the title. Cassie is a girl whose spirit and imagination belie the difficult circumstances that define the reality of her world.

While these multicultural stories may have specific applications, they are, first and foremost, simply good tales, well told. Stories affect us in much the same way that exposure to any other art form does. Children may grasp the essence but not the meat; details may be remembered incidentally or nuances not understood at the time. But, if a story has made an impression, it often provides a context to which they can refer back at any point later in life, reaching into their memory banks. Images held in reserve suddenly spring to the fore when needed, becoming like pieces of a puzzle that fill in the gaps to form a more complete picture of knowledge and understanding. Multicultural books for children may be specific to a time and place, with a setting that is very important or crucial to the story; they may have general appeal with simple timeless themes. Most importantly, they must portray the accomplishments, trials, and pleasures of childhood, making connections through common experiences and shared emotions, regardless of how they may be cloaked. ▲

ANNOTATED JOURNAL ARTICLES

Chance, Rosemary. "Voices from Diverse Cultures," *Emergency Librarian* (March/April 1995): 57-58.

The author reviews several young adult multicultural books. While values, traditions, and customs portrayed therein may be different from those of the youth that read the books, all young adults struggle with conflict in their lives. Reading these stories may help teens to realize that everyone experiences sorrow and joy, regardless of where they live.

Farris, Pamela J. "Exploring Multicultural Themes Through Picture Books," *Middle School Journal* (January 1995): 35-40.

This article states that teachers are responsible for creating common grounds for different cultures. Because many school libraries have small multicultural collections, picture books with a clear, direct, and short format present an understanding of different cultures to students of any age.

Lee, Mildred. "Building Bridges or Barriers?" *Horn Book Magazine* (March/April 1995): 233-36.

Multicultural books should tell stories of human events and the human condition to show the commonalities as well as the differences among people. Writing about another culture involves observing, understanding, and sharing its cultural traditions. Qualified people should review all multicultural literature for accuracy and sensitivity.

McElmeel, Sharron L. "Toward a Real Multiculturalism," *School Library Journal* (November 1993): 50.

Multicultural literature should familiarize readers with traditions and heritages, show children in present-day situations, and provide information about both differences and similarities. All children should be exposed to a great diversity of cultures and heritages so that they can learn to respect others and their ideas.

Smith, Karen Patricia. "The Multicultural Ethic and Connections to Literature for Children and Young Adults," *Library Trends (*Winter 1993): 340-53.

This article discusses the concept of multiculturalism and its relationship to literature for young people. The author points out that the definition of multiculturalism is changing to include any person whose lifestyle is different from the "mainstream." It is also important to have a clear understanding and strong appreciation for one's own culture. As teachers, we can no longer assume that this understanding is being taken care of at home.

ANNOTATED BIBLIOGRAPHY

Asian American

Hamanaka, Sheila. *Screen of Frogs: An Old Tale.* Orchard, 1993.

A frog, as large as a man and dressed in dripping green weeds, startles Koji and reminds him of all the natural beauty he could lose if he sells his land. Koji sells his other possessions to keep his land. The frogs, in gratitude, create a screen masterpiece to remind Koji of his commitment to the land.

McMahon, Patricia. *Chi-Hoon: A Korean Girl.* Caroline House, 1993.

On Monday, the principal of Chi-Hoon's school announces that the week's prize goes to the three students who are most dutiful and respectful. Chi-Hoon is disappointed that she isn't chosen, but she tries harder in the following weeks. One gets a glimpse of what it is like to be an eight-year-old Korean girl.

Say, Allen. *Tree of Cranes.* Houghton Mifflin, 1991.

Why is his mother acting so strangely? Why is she digging up the tree they planted when he was born? Finally, Mama places tiny cranes on the tree, along with candles. The boy discovers that this is part of a celebration Mama experienced when she was a young girl in California. According to custom, seven days before New Year's Day is a special day of peace and love. Thus the little boy experiences his first Christmas of peace and love in Japan.

Black American

Adler, David A. *A Picture Book of Rosa Parks.* Holiday House, 1993.

This well-illustrated biography of Rosa Parks, beginning with her childhood, is an eye-opening look at life for blacks in the South. The story tells of Rosa's part in the bus boycott and of her continued efforts on behalf of her race. Rosa Parks is a quiet but remarkable woman.

Binch, Caroline. *Gregory Cool.* Dial Books for Young Readers, 1994.

All-American Gregory visits relatives in Tobago for four weeks. Overwhelming heat, strange foods, and no television cause Gregory to wonder if he will survive his vacation. Then he meets his cousin Lennox, eventually learns how to be an island boy, and ends up liking this new way of life.

Pinkney, Andres Davis. *Alvin Ailey.* Hyperion Books for Children, 1993.

This book tells the story of the life of Alvin Ailey, including his interest in and knowledge of dance from an early age. Alvin started dancing seriously in 1949 with Lester Horton's Dance School in Los Angeles. This school admitted serious students of all races and taught the style of modern dance that Alvin loved. His work always honored the dignity of all black people.

Hispanic American

Dorros, Arthur. *Abuela.* Dutton Children's Books, 1991.

Colorful collage illustrations show the diversity of the location of this story (Manhattan, New York). Rosalba takes an imaginary journey flying through the skies above a park. The story has Spanish phrases sprinkled throughout and an underlying theme of family pride and love.

Reiser, Lynn. *Margaret and Margarita.* Greenwillow Books, 1993.

When they meet in the park, language is a barrier for the two mothers in this story. That is not the case for the two children, Margaret and Margarita. They teach each other words and develop a friendship. Both girls look forward to meeting in the park again. Simple bilingual text provides a word bridge for the girls and their mothers.

Soto, Gary. *Baseball in April & Other Stories.* Harcourt Brace Jovanovich, 1990.

A collection of short stories with vivid details of friendships, first love, and growing up Mexican American. Poet Gary Soto describes the trials and tribulations of middle-school-age kids in an engaging and personable style.

Winter, Jonah. *Diego.* Alfred A. Knopf, 1991.

This is the story of a famous Mexican artist, Jose Diego Rivera, who paints murals in public places. He has a deep respect for the common people of the world, the working class. His art is truly Mexican. The story has two texts, one in English and one in Spanish, with small but colorful illustrations.

Native American

Lourie, Peter. *Everglades: Buffalo Tiger and the River of Grass.* Boyds Mills Press, 1994.

The "river of grass," or the Everglades, located in south Florida, is home for the Miccosukee Indians. Buffalo Tiger, former chief of the Miccosukee, guides the author through the Everglades by airboat. Pollution, agriculture, and overdevelopment have damaged the Everglades. This book asks that we adhere to the Native Americans' sacred beliefs, to take only what we need and no more, while protecting the earth.

Martin, Rafe. *The Rough-Face Girl.* Putnam, 1992.

An Algonquin Cinderella tale of a rough-faced girl, scarred and burned from having to work too close to a fire. In this version, only the girl who could see the "invisible being" would become the Being's wife. The rough-faced girl sees the great beauty of the earth and the "invisible being" in all things. This is a different twist to a popular tale.

Masson, Jean Robert. *The Great Indian Chiefs: Cochise, Geronimo, Crazy Horse, Sitting Bull.* Barron's Educational Services, 1994.

The illustrator is given top billing on the title page, for good reason. Illustrations with concise text tell the story of the Apache and Sioux nations.

> Am I wrong to love my own law?
> Is it bad for me to have red skin?
> Because I am a Sioux?
> Because I was born where my father lived?
> Because I am ready to die for my people and my country?
> —*Sitting Bull*

BIBLIOGRAPHY

Asian American

Ashabranner, Brent, and Melissa Ashabranner. *Into a Strange Land: Unaccompanied Refugee Youth in America.* Dodd, Mead, 1987.

Behrens, June. *Gung Hay Fat Choy.* Childrens Press, 1982.

Brown, Tricia. *Chinese New Year.* Henry Holt, 1987.

Choi, Sook Nyul. *Year of Impossible Goodbyes.* Houghton Mifflin, 1991.

Coerr, Eleanor. *Sadako and the Thousand Paper Cranes.* G. P. Putnam's Sons, 1977.

Crew, Linda. *Children of the River.* Doubleday, 1989.

Davis, Daniel. *Behind Barbed Wire: The Imprisonment of Japanese Americans During World War II.* E. P. Dutton, 1982.

Fisher, Leonard Everett. *The Great Wall of China.* Macmillan, 1986.

Friedman, Ina R. *How My Parents Learned to Eat.* Houghton Mifflin, 1984.

Fritz, Jean. *Homesick: My Own Story.* Putnam, 1982.

Heyer, Marilee. *The Weaving of a Dream: A Chinese Folktale.* Viking Kestrel, 1986.

Hoyt-Goldsmith, Diane. *Hoang Anh: A Vietnamese American Boy.* Holiday House, 1992.

Huynh, Quang Nhuong. *The Land I Lost: Adventures of a Boy in Vietnam.* Harper & Row, 1982.

Leaf, Margaret. *Eyes of the Dragon.* Lothrop, Lee & Shepard, 1987.

Lord, Bette Bao. *In the Year of the Boar and Jackie Robinson.* Harper & Row, 1984.

Namioka, Lensey. *Yang the Youngest and His Terrible Ear.* Little, Brown, 1992.

Say, Allen. *El Chino.* Houghton Mifflin, 1990.

——. *A River Dream.* Houghton Mifflin, 1988.

Uchida, Yoshiko. *The Bracelet.* Philomel, 1993.

Waters, Kate. *Lion Dancer: Ernie Wan's Chinese New Year.* Scholastic, 1990.

Watkins, Yoko Kawashima. *So Far from the Bamboo Grove.* Lothrop, Lee & Shepard, 1986.

Yashima, Taro. *Crow Boy.* Puffin Books, 1976.

Yep, Laurence. *Child of the Owl.* Harper & Row, 1977.

——. *The Rainbow People.* Harper & Row, 1989.

Young, Ed. *Lon Po Po: A Red Riding Hood Story from China.* Philomel, 1989.

Black American

Aardema, Verna. *Bringing the Rain to Kapiti Plain: A Nandi Tale.* Dial Books for Young Readers, 1981.

——. *Who's in Rabbit's House?* Dial Press, 1977.

——. *Why Mosquitoes Buzz in People's Ears.* Dial Press, 1975.

Adler, David A. *A Picture Book of Martin Luther King, Jr.* Holiday House, 1989.

——. *A Picture Book of Rosa Parks.* Holiday House, 1993.

Adoff, Arnold. *All the Colors of the Race.* Lothrop, Lee & Shepard, 1982.

Carlstrom, Nancy White. *Baby-O.* Little, Brown, 1992.

Collier, James, and Christopher Collier. *With Every Drop of Blood.* Delacorte Press, 1994.

de Trevino, Elizabeth. *I, Juan de Pareja.* Farrar, Straus & Giroux, 1965.

Feelings, Muriel. *Jambo Means Hello: Swahili Alphabet Book.* Dial Books for Young Readers, 1974.

——. *Moja Means One: Swahili Counting Book.* Dial Books for Young Readers, 1971.

Ferris, Jerri. *Arctic Explorer: The Story of Matthew Henson.* Carolrhoda Books, 1989.

Flournoy, Valerie. *The Patchwork Quilt.* Dial Books for Young Readers, 1985.

Fox, Paula. *How Many Miles to Babylon?* Scholastic, 1967.

——. *Slave Dancer.* Dell, 1973.

Greene, Bette. *Philip Hall Likes Me. I Reckon Maybe.* Dial Press, 1974.

Grifalconi, Ann. *The Village of Round and Square Houses.* Little, Brown, 1986.

Haley, Gail E. *A Story, A Story.* Atheneum, 1970.

Hamilton, Virginia. *Anthony Burns: The Defeat and Triumph of a Fugitive Slave.* Alfred A. Knopf, 1988.

——. *The House of Dies Drear.* Macmillan, 1968.

——. *M. C. Higgins the Great.* Macmillan, 1974.

——. *The People Could Fly: American Black Folktales.* Alfred A. Knopf, 1985.

——. *Plain City.* Scholastic, 1993.

Hansen, Joyce. *Which Way Freedom.* Walker, 1986.

Harris, Joel Chandler. *Jump! The Adventures of Brer Rabbit*. Harcourt Brace Jovanovich, 1986.

Hoyt-Goldsmith, Diane. *Celebrating Kwanzaa*. Holiday House, 1993.

Johnson, Angelo. *Toning the Sweep*. Orchard, 1993.

Lester, Julius. *How Many Spots Does a Leopard Have?* Scholastic, 1989.

McKissack, Patricia. *Flossie and the Fox*. Dial Books for Young Readers, 1986.

———. *Louis Armstrong: Jazz Musician*. Enslow Publishers, 1991.

———. *Mirandy and Brother Wind*. Alfred A. Knopf, 1988.

Meltzer, Milton. *The Black Americans: A History in Their Own Words, 1619-1983*. Thomas Y. Crowell, 1984.

Monjo, N. *The Drinking Gourd*. Harper & Row, 1970.

Musgrove, Margaret. *Ashanti to Zulu: African Traditions*. Dial Press, 1976.

Myers, Walter Dean. *Scorpions*. Harper & Row, 1988.

Ringgold, Faith. *Tar Beach*. Crown, 1991.

Taylor, Mildred. *Let the Circle Be Unbroken*. Bantam Books, 1981.

———. *Roll of Thunder, Hear My Cry*. Dial Press, 1976.

Hispanic American

Ada, Alma Flor. *My Name Is Maria Isabel*. Atheneum, 1993.

Anaya, Rudolfo. *The Farolitos of Christmas*. Hyperion, 1995.

Ashabranner, Brent. *Children of the Maya: A Guatemalan Indian Odyssey*. Dodd, Mead, 1986.

Bierhorst, John, ed. *Doctor Coyote: A Native American Aesop's Fables*. Macmillan, 1987.

Brimner, Larry Dane. *A Migrant Family*. Lerner, 1992.

Brusca, Maria Cristina. *On the Pampas*. Henry Holt, 1991.

Buss, Fran Leeper, and Daisy Cubias. *Journey of the Sparrows*. Lodestar, 1991.

Cameron, Ann. *The Most Beautiful Place in the World*. Alfred A. Knopf, 1993.

Castañeda, Omar S. *Abuela's Weave*. Lee & Low Books, 1993.

Clark, Ann Nolan. *Secret of the Andes*. Puffin Books, 1984.

DeStefano, Susan. *Chico Mendes: Fight for the Forest*. Henry Holt, 1992.

Drucker, Malka. *Frida Kahlo: Torment and Triumph in Her Life and Art*. Bantam Books, 1991.

Ets, Marie Hall, and Aurora Labastida. *Nine Days to Christmas: A Story of Mexico*. Viking, 1959.

Greene, Carol. *Roberto Clemente: Baseball Superstar*. Childrens Press, 1991.

———. *Simón Bolívar: South American Liberator*. Childrens Press, 1989.

Hoyt-Goldsmith, Diane. *Day of the Dead: A Mexican-American Celebration*. Holiday House, 1994.

Hurwitz, Johanna. *Class President*. Morrow Junior Books, 1990.

Kroll, Virginia. *Pink Paper Swans*. William B. Eerdmans, 1994.

Krumgold, Joseph. *. . . And Now Miguel*. Thomas Y. Crowell, 1953.

Lasky, Kathryn. *Days of the Dead*. Hyperion Books for Children, 1994.

Marzollo, Jean. *The Best Friends Club*. Scholastic, 1990.

Mikaelsen, Ben. *Sparrow Hawk Red*. Hyperion Books for Children, 1993.

Mora, Pat. *Pablo's Tree*. Macmillan, 1994.

Mora, Pat, and Charles Ramirez Berg. *The Gift of the Poinsettia*. Arte Publico Press, 1995.

O'Dell, Scott. *Carlota*. Houghton Mifflin, 1981.

———. *The King's Fifth*. Houghton Mifflin, 1966.

Politi, Leo. *Song of the Swallows*. Charles Scribner's Sons, 1949.

Reed, Lynn Rowe. *Pedro, His Perro, and the Alphabet Sombrero*. Hyperion Books for Children, 1995.

Sinnott, Susan. *Extraordinary Hispanic Americans*. Childrens Press, 1991.

Soto, Gary. *Canto Familiar*. Harcourt Brace Jovanovich, 1995.

———. *Too Many Tamales*. G. P. Putnam's Sons, 1993.

Native American

Aliki. *Corn Is Maize*: *The Gift of the Indians*. Thomas Y. Crowell, 1976.

Ashabranner, Brent. *To Live in Two Worlds: American Indian Youth Today*. Dodd, Mead, 1984.

Baylor, Byrd. *Hawk, I'm Your Brother*. Charles Scribner's Sons, 1976.

———. *When Clay Sings*. Charles Scribner's Sons, 1972.

Bierhorst, John, ed. *The Whistling Skeleton: American Indian Tales of the Supernatural*. Four Winds Press, 1982.

Bulla, Clyde Robert. *Conquista!* Thomas Y. Crowell, 1978.

Curtis, Edward S. *The Girl Who Married a Ghost and Other Tales from the North American Indian*. Four Winds Press, 1978.

dePaola, Tomie. *The Legend of the Bluebonnet*. Putnam, 1983.

Esbensen, Barbara Juster, ed. *The Star Maiden*. Little, Brown, 1988.

Freedman, Russell. *Buffalo Hunt*. Holiday House, 1988.

———. *Indian Chiefs*. Holiday House, 1987.

———. *An Indian Winter*. Holiday House, 1992.

George, Jean Craighead. *The Talking Earth*. Harper & Row, 1983.

Goble, Paul. *Buffalo Woman*. Bradbury Press, 1984.

———. *The Gift of the Sacred Dog*. Bradbury Press, 1980.

———. *The Girl Who Loved Wild Horses*. Bradbury Press, 1978.

———. *Iktomi and the Boulder: A Plains Indian Story*. Orchard, 1988.

Hobbs, Will. *Bearstone*. Atheneum, 1989.

Martin, Bill, and John Archambault. *Knots on a Counting Rope*. Henry Holt, 1987.

McDermott, Gerald. *Raven*. Harcourt Brace Jovanovich, 1993.

Mowat, Farley. *Lost in the Barrens*. McClelland & Stewart, 1966.

O'Dell, Scott. *Black Star, Bright Star*. Houghton Mifflin, 1988.

———. *Sing Down the Moon*. Houghton Mifflin, 1970.

Paulsen, Gary. *Dogsong*. Bradbury Press, 1988.

Speare, Elizabeth George. *The Sign of the Beaver*. Houghton Mifflin, 1983.

Steptoe, John. *The Story of Jumping Mouse*. Lothrop, Lee & Shepard, 1984.

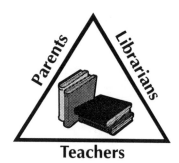

Parents
Librarians
Teachers

Chapter 7

All Kinds of Poetry

OVERVIEW

Poetry has been called the language of emotions; however, there is an elusive quality about poetry that defies exact definition. It is not so much how we feel about poetry as how poetry makes us feel. Poetry has the power to elicit rich sensory images and deep emotional responses. Poetry can only happen when the poem and the reader connect. Poetry for children differs little from poetry for adults, except that it comments on life in ways and proportions that are meaningful for children. The topics in appropriate poetry should pertain to children's experiences, with the emotional enticement reflecting the real feelings and concerns of childhood.

Modern poetry for children often reflects the despair of struggling to grow up in America today. Topics such as latchkey children, divorce, and single-parent families are evident in more recent poetry. However, poetry should also include the humorous, fanciful, and imaginative as well. A variety of forms, such as ballads, narrative, lyric, limerick, free verse, haiku, and concrete poetry should be included in a poetry collection for children.

GUIDED READING QUESTIONS

1. Do the illustrations impose a viewpoint or an interpretation of the poetry? Are there illustrations for every poem?

2. Do you prefer an anthology or a book of poems all by the same author?

3. Do you find poems about current social problems? Are they effective?

4. Do you find poetry in different forms, such as haiku, limericks, ballads, and so on?

5. Does any one poet or poem develop your sensory images?

6. Does any one poet or poem inspire particularly strong images or emotions?

JOURNAL ARTICLE

Children's Poetry: Journeying Beyond the Road Less Traveled

Think of it as psychology without the guilt, songs without the music, art without the illustration.

811 is a lonely number. Sandwiched between the heavily traveled sports and recreation books, and the history/biography aisle (crowded with kids looking for term paper topics), children's poetry meekly exists. Here sits a volume of Lear that hasn't circulated since 1980 and the unattractive and often intimidating anthology of "best loved" (by whom?) children's poetry.

While poetry may not seem to be the most appealing area for children to explore, that can change as quickly as the slithy toves can gyre and gimble. All it takes is for adults to realize this and set youngsters onto the road less traveled.

At the Milwaukee Public Library branch where I worked, far too often the stacks in "poetry row" were clear of traffic, almost daring some child to browse. Unless a teacher had assigned a project, the kids shied away—with one exception. It seemed every third child was looking for Shel Silverstein's *Where the Sidewalk Ends* (1974) or *A Light in the Attic* (1981, both HarperCollins). The prince of contemporary nonsense verse had them all under a spell, understandably so. But aside from his humor, and the occasional holiday poetry, kids would rarely look beyond.

By Sharon Korbeck. Reprinted with permission from *School Library Journal* (April 1995), pages 43-44. Sharon Korbeck is formerly a Children's/YA librarian at Milwaukee Public Library.

Obstacles in the Road

Why has children's poetry gotten such a negative rap among the very crowd it's designed for? Poetry is often misunderstood by adults. That rubs off on children. The fear of not understanding it is far too common. That's why nonsense verse thrives; it doesn't profess to *mean* anything, though underlying currents are often present.

Children's poetry especially should be addressed with verve and fun, rather than intimidation. As librarians and teachers, we need to set this pattern. Don't analyze it too much, but rather enjoy it for what it is—a unique presentation of timeless and universal topics. Think of it as psychology without the guilt, songs without the music, art without the illustration.

The Road Paved with Good Intentions

By presenting children's poetry in the library and classrooms, we open the highway of possibilities. But educators aren't the only ones doing that. Poets and anthologists are realizing that the world is changing and so must literature and poetry. Over the past decade especially, children's poetry has matured, or at least the view of what constitutes it has.

While nonsense and "fun" verse is still thriving and always will, children's poetry is taking on a more serious face in step with changing, and more demanding, social times. Adults mustn't fear that change, but rather welcome it.

Once taboo or more serious topics were reserved for adult readers. Now numerous anthologies for children use poetry to illustrate human rights, environmental concerns, even AIDS and economics. Sometimes a brief poetic snapshot provides a much more vivid portrait than a nonfiction book can.

Anthologies are wonderful for several reasons. They expose children to a variety of poets, mixing the old and the new. They bring contemporary and historical voices together, spanning decades and centuries in a single thought or vision.

They create continuity of theme, aiding the teacher or librarian in providing a book on a particular topic. Anthologies also allow children to read poems in a context that may aid understanding. The editor assembles the selections around a theme; together they take on a power not always evident to children reading a stand-alone poem.

Paul Janeczko's *Looking for Your Name* (Orchard, 1993) is one fine example. In this dynamic YA collection, contemporary poets speak of nuclear accidents, patriotism, and family. Their words are honest and striking. Photos aren't necessary since the words powerfully illustrate the problems of today.

In Bruno Navasky's *Festival in My Heart: Poems by Japanese Children* (Abrams, 1993), kindergartners through seventh graders share their insights about subjects as varied as Hiroshima and Buddha, as well as the simpler essences of frogs, trees, and ants. Kids pull no punches, and these poems are from the heart and from the hip. Why seek out the words of others when much of what flows from a child's mind and mouth is quite poetic?

Barbara Brenner's *The Earth Is Painted Green* (Scholastic, 1993) is a collection aimed at younger readers. Its bright, colorful pages invite children to read more about the earth, nature, animals—fostering a greater respect and awareness of our world. Humorous and more pensive pieces live comfortably together here in this inviting, browsable book.

One of the best collections in recent years, however, is Nora Panzer's *Celebrate America: In Poetry and Art* (Hyperion, 1994). Giving children a well-rounded sense of what it means to be an American (or an African American, Polish American, Asian American, etc.), this collection triumphs in its rich selections. Do you know where Emma Lazarus's now-famous poem inscribed on the Statue of Liberty came from? What about the Preamble to the U.S. Constitution? Do you recall Maya Angelou's resounding lyrics at President Clinton's inauguration? Those words truly echo with America's spirit. It is here that the voices of e. e. cummings, Walt Whitman, and James Weldon Johnson come together in peace and harmony—which is one message this collection sends loud and clear—let's all live together and celebrate our fine, richly patterned heritage. Artwork in a variety of mediums from the National Museum of American Art at the Smithsonian Institution enhances the title, prompting repeated perusals.

Pass It On: African-American Poetry for Children (Scholastic, 1993) is a beautiful offering selected by Wade Hudson. Floyd Cooper's soft yet striking images give children of all races an introduction to the classic African American poets— Hughes, Dunbar, Giovanni, and Brooks, among others. One of the key aspects of the book is that it masquerades as a picture book, and that's sometimes important in getting a child to look at a book. It doesn't look intimidating, but rather is thoroughly engaging.

Nikki Giovanni's *Knoxville, Tennessee* (Scholastic, 1994) isn't an anthology but rather an example of how one poem is presented as a picture book. It works extremely well with Larry Johnson's vibrant paintings of the African American experience. Another similar presentation is Maya Angelou's *Life Doesn't Frighten Me* (Stewart, Tabori & Chang, 1993), illustrated with the graffiti of late street-artist Jean-Michel Basquiat. Both the author and the illustrator have had hard lives, a fact harshly evident in words and illustrations.

These two books are excellent examples of how presenting poetry in different formats can increase interest and readability for children. Angelou and Giovanni are two of the finest poets of any race or time, but perhaps may not have been given much attention by children because of how their works were presented.

James Berry's *Celebration Song* (S. & S., 1994) is a nativity song/poem set against a Caribbean background. It tells of Jesus' "born-day" as a happening event, one "alive in jubilation." Louise Brierley's watercolors are awash with the emotion of the day and the cadence and feeling of celebration. Poetry is a delightful way to present nonfiction; this offering is unusual and appropriate for presenting Christmas, music, poetry, or simply a cultural story.

Lori Carlson's *Cool Salsa: Bilingual Poems on Growing Up Latino in the United States* (Holt, 1994) comes as a bright spot, filling a somewhat narrowing void in poetry for young people. Oscar Hijuelos introduces the volume, which features English and Spanish versions of the poems. These are the poets' words of identity, understanding, oppression, and honesty—attempting to shatter stereotypes while celebrating family and recalling a powerful and painful history. The poets profess (as Ana Castillo's poem shows), "We are left with one final resolution . . . we are going forward. There is no going back."

While children's poetry and the publishing world's presentation of it have matured, there's still a lot of good nonsense verse out there, as well there should be. Even if it's only a brief stroll down the poetry road, it's well worth it.

Myra Cohn Livingston says in her book *Climb into the Bell Tower* (Harper-Collins, 1990; o.p.), "Nonsense, in whatever form, drawing or words, is the escape hatch from the trials of life." How true, and how wonderful that children can look forward to such gems as David Booth's *Doctor Knickerbocker and Other Rhymes* (Ticknor & Fields, 1993), a playful, Goreyesque collection; *A. Nonny Mouse Writes Again* (Knopf, 1993), a fun collection of anonymous verse selected by Jack Prelutsky, and with his own *Something Big Has Been Here* (Greenwillow, 1990), Prelutsky is hot on Silverstein's silly trail.

Colin McNaughton's *Making Friends with Frankenstein: A Book of Monstrous Poems and Pictures* (Candlewick, 1994) is a recent romp that purveys a wonderful use of silliness, attractive page design, and wacky illustrations. The poems are short, punchy, and sometimes irreverently goofy. While such silliness isn't entirely original, McNaughton's cyclops, aliens, and monsters are all resident experts at tickling the minds of middle graders. It's great fun, especially for reading aloud.

There is too much wonderment in children's poetry for it to get lost amid Dewey's dusty aisles and an adult's opinion of what's interesting, worthwhile, and comprehensive. As librarians and educators, we must reopen the windows of wonder with both contemporary and absurd verse. The selection may not exactly be endless, but progress is being made.

Just get the right pictures and words into the hands of the inquisitive, or even the doubting, child and see what transpires. It may take a few tries or even some creative approaches, but it will be well worth the effort. It may even open your eyes to what's out there . . . and what's missing.

Booktalk it, display it, promote it—do whatever you can to introduce children to the road less traveled. It will make all the difference. ▲

ANNOTATED JOURNAL ARTICLES

Cart, Michael. "The Poet's Question—A Conversation with Myra Cohn Livingston," *Booklist* (June 1995): 1745.

"Is formal poetry dead?" asks Cart. Livingston states that just because a poem is published doesn't mean it is good. She says that anyone who does research can write authentic poetry about any culture. Poetry for children must speak to them and enable them to see things in ways they've never seen before. Poetry must appeal not only to the head but also to the body. A good poem will grab your sense of rhythm.

Harms, Jeanne, and Lucille Lettow. "Supporting Environmental Education Through Poetry," *Youth Services in Libraries* (Winter 1995): 167-71.

"Poetry can foster awareness, identification, appreciation, and a sense of stewardship of the environment through its sharp, intense confrontations with ideas," say the authors. The sound elements of poetry can entice students to return again and again until the messages about the environment are committed to memory.

Meier, Daniel. "Books in the Classroom," *Horn Book Magazine* (July/August 1988): 524-26.

"As I read a poem, my students listen for noise. They listen for quiet. They listen for humor. They listen for sadness. Poetry, close to a child's ear, speaks to his or her formidable powers of oral language and invites the child to become an active listener," says Meier. When poetry is read aloud, reading no longer is a mechanical process; it becomes drama or theater.

Webre, Elizabeth C. "Learning About Science Through Poetry." *Teaching K-8* (February 1995): 50-51.

"Science teachers are constantly searching for ways to instill interest in science and have students relate new learning to everyday life," states the author. She then illustrates many ways to do just that, using a poetry book about insects.

Wilson, Patricia J., and Karen Kutiper. "Beyond Silverstein and Prelutsky: Enhancing and Promoting the Elementary and Middle School Poetry Collection," *Youth Services in Libraries* (Spring 1994): 273-79.

"Exposure to poetry in its many forms and with its sometimes playful and sometimes sophisticated uses of language can only enhance children's literacy development. This exposure must be thoughtfully and carefully planned," state the authors. Interest in poetry begins with the library media specialist, who builds a rich, inviting collection of poetry and then encourages teachers and students to explore and appreciate poetry's unique contributions to the world of literature.

ANNOTATED BIBLIOGRAPHY

Carle, Eric. *Dragons Dragons and Other Creatures That Never Were*. Philomel, 1991.

Dragons Dragons is a companion volume to *Animals Animals*. Laura Whipple has compiled a collection of poems about dragons and other fantastic creatures. Eric Carle's rich illustrations will attract students to read further.

Carlson, Lori M., ed. *Cool Salsa: Bilingual Poems on Growing Up Latino in the United States.* Henry Holt, 1994.

A wide variety of poems about life in two cultures, presented in both English and Spanish. Topics include school and school days, home and homeland, memories, hard times, and time to party. Some sophisticated subjects, but all are written passionately.

Frost, Robert. *Stopping by Woods on a Snowy Evening.* Illustrated by Susan Jeffers. E. P. Dutton, 1978.
Wintry New England scenes illustrate this famous Robert Frost poem. This is a wonderful version to share with the family.

McPhail, David. *Pigs Aplenty, Pigs Galore.* Dutton Children's Books, 1993.
The story of an author reading quietly, hearing noises, and discovering that many pigs have taken over his house. They eat, play, work, and make a huge mess. The entire story is in rhyme and the artwork enhances the book.

Singer, Marilyn. *It's Hard to Read a Map with a Beagle on Your Lap.* Henry Holt, 1993.
Humorous poems about dogs accompanied by equally humorous illustrations, sure to be popular with students.

Steig, Jeanne. *Alpha Beta Chowder.* HarperCollins, 1992.
A poem for every letter of the alphabet. Each poem contains words beginning with the same letter. The illustrations add to the fun and merriment.

BIBLIOGRAPHY

General

Adoff, Arnold. *All the Colors of the Race.* Lothrop, Lee & Shepard, 1982.

Benet, Rosemary, and Stephen Vincent Benet. *A Book of Americans.* Henry Holt, 1987.

Booth, David. *'Til All the Stars Have Fallen: A Collection of Poems for Children.* Viking, 1990.

Brown, Marc. *Party Rhymes.* E. P. Dutton, 1988.

de Regniers, Beatrice S. *Sing a Song of Popcorn: Every Child's Book of Poems.* Scholastic, 1988.

Esbensen, Barbara J. *Who Shrank My Grandmother's House? Poems of Discovery.* HarperCollins, 1992.

Ferris, Helen. *Favorite Poems Old and New.* Doubleday, 1957.

Frost, Robert. *Stopping by Woods on a Snowy Evening.* E. P. Dutton, 1978.

Hall, Donald, ed. *The Oxford Book of Children's Verse in America.* Oxford University Press, 1985.

Hopkins, Lee Bennett. *Surprises.* Harper & Row, 1984.

———. *More Surprises.* Harper & Row, 1987.

Kennedy, X. J. *The Kite That Braved Old Orchard Beach: Year-Round Poems for Young People.* Macmillan, 1991.

———. *Talking Like the Rain: A First Book of Poems.* Little, Brown, 1992.

Larrick, Nancy. *Piping Down the Valleys Wild.* Delacorte Press, 1985.

Livingston, Myra Cohn. *Why Am I Grown So Cold? Poems of the Unknowable.* Macmillan, 1982.

Longfellow, Henry Wadsworth. *Hiawatha.* Dial Books for Young Readers, 1983.

Merriam, Eve. *You Be Good and I'll Be Night: Jump-on-the-Bed Poems.* Morrow Junior Books, 1988.

Noyes, Alfred. *The Highwayman.* Oxford University Press, 1987.

Pomerantz, Charlotte. *If I Had a Paka: Poems in Eleven Languages.* Greenwillow Books, 1993.

Prelutsky, Jack. *The Random House Book of Poetry for Children.* Random House, 1983.

———. *Read-Aloud Rhymes for the Very Young.* Alfred A. Knopf, 1986.

Schwartz, Alvin. *And the Green Grass Grew All Around: Folk Poetry from Everyone.* Harper-Collins, 1992.

Service, Robert W. *The Cremation of Sam McGee.* Greenwillow Books, 1987.

———. *The Shooting of Dan McGrew.* Godine, 1988.

Silverstein, Shel. *Where the Sidewalk Ends.* Harper & Row, 1974.

Stevenson, Robert Louis. *A Child's Garden of Verses.* Derrydale Books, 1986.

Thayer, Ernest Lawrence. *Casey at the Bat.* G. P. Putnam's Sons, 1988.

Viorst, Judith. *If I Were in Charge of the World and Other Worries: Poems for Children and Their Parents.* Macmillan, 1981.

Yolen, Jane. *Bird Watch.* Philomel, 1990.

Humorous

Belloc, Hilaire. *Matilda, Who Told Such Dreadful Lies.* Alfred A. Knopf, 1992.

Ciardi, John. *The Hopeful Trout and Other Limericks.* Houghton Mifflin, 1989.

Lear, Edward. *Of Pelicans and Pussycats: Poems and Limericks.* Dial Books for Young Readers, 1990.

Lobel, Arnold. *The Book of Pigericks: Pig Limericks.* Harper & Row, 1983.

McNaughton, Colin. *Making Friends with Frankenstein.* Candlewick Press, 1994.

Nash, Ogden. *The Adventures of Isabel.* Little, Brown, 1991.

Prelutsky, Jack. *For Laughing Out Loud: Poems to Tickle Your Funnybone.* Alfred A. Knopf, 1991.

———. *The New Kid on the Block.* Greenwillow Books, 1984.

———. *Poems of A. Nonny Mouse.* Alfred A. Knopf, 1989.

———. *Ride a Purple Pelican.* Greenwillow Books, 1980.

———. *Something Big Has Been Here.* Greenwillow Books, 1990.

Steig, Jeanne. *Consider the Lemming.* Farrar, Straus & Giroux, 1988.

Tripp, Wallace. *A Great Big, Ugly Man Came Up and Tied His Horse to Me: A Book of Nonsense Verse.* Little, Brown, 1974.

Westcott, Nadine Bernard. *The Lady with the Alligator Purse.* Little, Brown, 1988.

———. *Never Take a Pig to Lunch.* Orchard, 1994.

Yolen, Jane. *How Beastly: A Menagerie of Nonsense Poems.* Wordsong, 1980.

———. *Street Rhymes Around the World.* Boyds Mills Press, 1992.

Animals

Fisher, Aileen. *Rabbits, Rabbits.* Harper & Row, 1983.

Fleischman, Paul. *Joyful Noise: Poems for Two Voices.* Harper & Row, 1988.

Lewis, J. Patrick. *A Hippopotamusn't and Other Animal Verses*. Dial Books for Young Readers, 1990.

Livingston, Myra Cohn. *If the Owl Calls Again: A Collection of Owl Poems*. Macmillan, 1990.

Prelutsky, Jack. *Tyrannosaurus Was a Beast*. Greenwillow Books, 1988.

Whipple, Laura. *Eric Carle's Animals Animals*. Philomel, 1989.

Miscellaneous

Brewton, John E. *In the Witch's Kitchen: Poems for Halloween*. Thomas Y. Crowell, 1980.

Hazeltine, Alice Isabel, and Elva Smith. *The Year Around: Poems for Children*. Books for Libraries Press, 1973.

Higginson, William J. *In the Eyes of the Cat: Japanese Poetry for All Seasons*. Henry Holt, 1992.

———. *Wind in the Long Grass: A Collection of Haiku*. Simon & Schuster, 1991.

Lindbergh, Reeve. *The Midnight Farm*. Dial Books for Young Readers, 1987.

Livingston, Myra Cohn. *Celebrations*. Holiday House, 1985.

———. *Poems for Jewish Holidays*. Holiday House, 1986.

Prelutsky, Jack. *It's Thanksgiving*. Greenwillow Books, 1982.

———. *It's Valentine's Day*. Greenwillow Books, 1983.

Thomas, Dylan. *A Child's Christmas in Wales*. Holiday House, 1985.

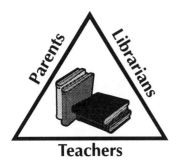

Chapter 8

Science Fiction and Fantasy

OVERVIEW

The science fiction and fantasy genre has existed for more than 100 years. It helps to believe that the scenes and personalities created by the author are genuine. This is often difficult, though, and may be one reason why readers either love or hate science fiction and fantasy. Also, it is sometimes perplexing to identify fantasy, because it can be so similar to science fiction. Science fiction is often considered a subgenre of fantasy. Both usually concern the conflict between good and evil, but science fiction accentuates scientific principles and technological discoveries. Time travel, as an element in fantasy, has recently become predominant.

This genre of books is popular for a variety of reasons. Enigmatic surroundings, imaginary languages, inconceivable wizardry, and bizarre beasts fascinate readers. The struggle between good and evil, linked with the unfamiliar and a hearty measure of dangerous discord, kindles the imagination. These books are often difficult to put down.

GUIDED READING QUESTIONS

1. Would you classify the book as science fiction or fantasy? Why?

2. Do you like or dislike these kinds of books? How do you feel about this book in particular?

3. Was the book suspenseful?

4. Would the book be frightening or too intense for a child?

5. Were the characters developed?

6. Was there an actual plot?

From *The Reading Connection.* © 1997. Libraries Unlimited. (800) 237-6124.

Future Tense: Science Fiction Confronts the New Science

The "Tomorrow Makers," Grant Fjermedal's term,[1] refers to scientists engaged in projects at the frontiers of their fields—robotics, genetic engineering, and artificial intelligence. The visionary, futuristic work of these people often appears to be the stuff of science fiction—and naturally, because the new science excites the imagination, it is fertile ground for the speculation of science fiction writers. Extrapolation from known scientific facts and advances in technology are hallmarks of the genre; as Stewart Brand says, science and science fiction "are so blurred together they are practically one intellectual activity."[2]

Whereas much of the older science fiction conveyed a tone of the paramilitary, the pseudo-science, or the fantastic, many recently published juvenile and young adult science fiction titles contain an emphasis on and a connection with technological breakthroughs of our time— a concern with the dangers of technological developments as they pertain to the future of humankind, rather than the danger of an alien technology brought to bear on human life. Writers of SF stories for young readers—and many of today's SF authors are women—create youthful heroes of both sexes who journey to the far edges of science and the universe in entertaining stories which, by echoing progress reported by newspapers and scientific journals, also inform young readers. These books' connection with the new science allows young readers opportunities to journey, along with the young protagonists, to the world of the "Tomorrow Makers."

Genetic Engineering

The production, by scientists from Johns Hopkins and Auburn University in 1988, of a genetically altered carp that could grow up to 20 percent faster than a normal carp, was just one recent example of the developing uses of genetic engineering. Gene mixing/splicing has since been achieved in microbes and in plants, rodents and livestock. People have used applied biotechnology, such as fermentation or baking with yeast, since ancient times; but recent advances have enabled scientists working in recombinant DNA or gene splicing to remove genes from one organism and attach them to the DNA of another organism. A 1980 ruling by the U.S. Supreme Court permits companies to patent new forms of life.

While such scientific breakthroughs hold a promise for improved crops and better livestock to enhance our food supply, or for the development of cures for diseases, the advent of biotechnology has spawned a hot debate over its potentially harmful effects. Concerns are being voiced, for example, about the possibility of an escape of mutant strains which might result in environmental damage, or their deliberate use in biological warfare—or even in the creation of a race of superhumans.

By Janice Antczak. Reprinted with permission from *School Library Journal* (January 1990), pages 29-32. Janice Antczak is Professor of Literature and Library Science at Brookdale Community College, Lincroft, NJ.

All of these issues are now on the pages of juvenile/young adult science fiction books. Several published in the late '80s incorporate biotechnology into their plots. One such example is Pamela Sargent's *Alien Child*, set at the Kwalung-Ibarra Institute. The main characters, Nita and Sven (products of the Institute's work in *in vitro* fertilization and cryonics), are brought forth from the "cold room" and nurtured by the aliens Llipel and Llare. Nita and Sven represent a benign use of genetic engineering—the creation and storage of embryos to be presented, at the right time, to loving parents—but the author's message is decidedly mixed. By juxtaposing Nita and Sven's awakening knowledge of the horror and destruction brought upon the Earth by biological warfare, Sargent's thoughtful work explores both the hopes and the hazards of biotechnology.

In Annabel and Edgar Johnson's *The Danger Quotient*, genetic engineering sustains life 130 years after War Three. The novel takes place at a time when remnants of human civilization survive in deep shelter to avoid radiation and ozone depletion; biotechnology is necessary to support and create life. Continued existence is possible only by the "ingenuity of genetic engineers like Helmet Eddinger," who the author says has developed "new strains of hydroponic fruit, long-grain wheat that heads out in ten days, cows that produce triplets [and] superkids concocted in the test tube . . . to give us extra brain power." One of Eddinger's genetic hybrids, K/C-4(SCI), is designed to solve the problems threatening continued survival, but there is one design flaw. These superkids don't have a chance to enjoy longevity; premature aging in their teens claims them before they reach their early twenties. As Sargent does in *Alien Child*, the Johnsons provide readers plenty of opportunities to speculate about the use of biotechnology and how it might have an impact in the future.

Laurence Yep, known for his books about the Chinese-American experience, uses genetic engineering as the premise for the plot in *Monster Makers, Inc.* In this adventure, Rob Kincaid's father hopes to make a fortune with MMI—"The best in genetic engineering." Mr. Kincaid has come up with some strange creations already, including an Adelbaran chomper (a giant worm used to aerate farm soil), a line of prehistoric pets (baby ankylosaurs and mini-mastodons), but his prize is a mini-Godzilla, which he had hoped would be a hit with tourists. "People out here are still leery of genetic engineering," says Kincaid, "but once we show them it's safe, we'll be rich."

Yep weaves a tale in which Rob and Shandi, a spunky young heiress, retrieve a rampaging Godzilla and fight nefarious aliens to once more make the planet Carefree worthy of its name. The lighthearted banter of the characters establishes a tone for the novel in which industrial intrigue and sabotage lend excitement. Genetic engineering is not seriously questioned here, but is treated as a facet of technology to be explored for both practical application and for profit.

John Forrester's *Bestiary Mountain* and *The Secret of the Round Beast* (the first two books in a trilogy concluded by *The Forbidden Beast*) each include genetic engineering as part of life after the chemical wars of the 2130s. Forrester writes that in the world of *Bestiary Mountain*, "too much feeling for plants and animals was something to be watched, [for] humankind had conquered the animals in the final wars that came after genetic engineering had given animals minds and hands. . . ." Since that time genetic engineering in the space stations orbiting Luna produced "the animals bred in moon labs . . . for hunting by the workers. There had been lion-rams and rhino buffalo, tigers with horns, anything the geneticists could dream up and splice together out of DNA."

Ryland and Tava Langstrom are genetic engineers who have been outlawed for their work. Ryland wishes to continue to study the dune bears (the remaining beasts of the colony world) and the DNA of telepathic animals—study which is forbidden by the government. Tava steals an earth-rocket outfitted as an exploratory genetics unit and returns back to Old Earth. There, she develops Kana—half-cat, half-human boy—as she works to restore animals "from cryogenic DNA banks on the moon islands" and to seek out animals she doesn't have in storage to "add to their numbers by cloning."

Forrester's second volume, *The Secret of the Round Beast*, continued the conflict. Other hybrid creatures—like the foxal, and various cat hybrids—emerge. On one side are the Langstroms, who represent the benevolent aspect of genetic engineering; on the other, Gorid Hawxhurst, the evil scientist whose objective is the creation of hybrids for the hunt. (His name suggests his brutal, sadistic nature.) More serious in tone than Yep's *Monster Makers, Inc.,* Forrester's trilogy still maintains a sense of adventure and romance, as it explores the conflict of Old Earth and its colonies caused by genetic manipulation.

Artificial Intelligence

Scientists in artificial intelligence (AI) laboratories around the globe are exploring the idea of downloading the contents of human brains into robotic bodies. At the Massachusetts Institute of Technology, Danny Hillis is working on a "connection machine," a non-sequential computer which would be able to do millions of things at once—more like a human brain than a mere computer. MIT's Carl Hewitt is exploring ways in which these parallel computers can advance the development of artificial intelligence to aid human beings

to control their use of planet Earth. AI units would thus become the "caretakers" of the human race. In England, Kerry Joels, a fellow of the Royal Astronomical Society, believes robots will be made to look more like humans, as do the androids in *Blade Runner* and *The Terminator*.

Engineer Charles Lecht, of Lecht Sciences, Inc., claims that biochip technology could free the human race. Lecht, Hans Moravec of Pittsburgh's Carnegie-Mellon University, and Marvin Minsky of MIT envision "artificial experience" whereby one could, via headsets and sensors, explore the world without ever leaving home. Or, through the use of holography, a person living on the East Coast could dine with friends on the West Coast—or one could decorate one's home with luxuries. All of this raises questions at once basic and fantastic: What is real? What is life? What is a human being?

Recent novels suggest that AI may be one of the more frequently used aspects of the new technology in science fiction for young readers. In the first two books of Forrester's trilogy, many of these ideas become part of the story. Some of *Bestiary Mountain's* Overones, the robotic guardians of Old Earth and its colonies, are faceless and machinelike, but newer units are "partly organic and partly electronic creations." In *The Secret of the Round Beast*, the Overones have a technology which allows them to copy the neural imprints of humans and duplicate their thoughts: "a system called Software Input, which allows brain-to-brain processing." These elements of the novel sound much like the downloading of brain contents discussed by the AI scientists. Forrester's robots and androids, who once were to be soldiers and miners, the "caretakers," are now in charge. In an aside, Forrester says the robots "make wonderful bureaucrats" and are "perfect in middle management."

Ryland Langstrom discusses this with Marian Lytal, an engineer designing organic robots. "You're making the units more human?" Ryland asks. Marian replies, "It might be dangerous—as they get nearer us, they will understand us better. And they might decide to replace us." The robots/androids become obsessed with re-design and self-improvement, and their mission becomes one "to eliminate selected humans, just as fast as they think they can do without them." Forrester's novel echoes what Earl Joseph said, that "the door has been opened with artificial intelligence and recombinant DNA . . . There is some possibility of creating a human race that will be beyond humans."[3]

These ideas are also found in Sargent's *Alien Child*. The Kwalung-Ibarra Institute depends on robots and AI for its continued existence. "The intelligence's circuits were embedded in the walls and floors of the Institute. Through robots, the artificial intelligence maintained the Institute and the garden. . . ." Nita realizes that her life "depended on the Institute's artificial intelligence and the technology that served it. . . ." When she and Sven journey outside the Institute to find other humans, they travel to the nearest city and find that the only survivor is another artificial intelligence which says it has searched all over the Earth and has seen no other trace of humans. As Nita and Sven talk to it about the destruction, Nita realizes that "her people had used even the minds that served them to destroy themselves."

Other authors include AI in their vision of the future. Louise Lawrence, in *Moonwind*, has a cybernetic intelligence caring for Bethkan for the 10,000 orbital years she has been stranded on the moon. In George Zebrowski's *The Stars Will Speak*, each student is "given a personal AI" and "will pursue various subjects. The AI or a visiting scientist may occasionally suggest an assignment."

Ardath Mayhar's *A Place of Silver Silence* reflects Charles Lecht's ideas concerning biochip technology. Selected pairs of young people are "Linked" using "technology that came into being with the prototypes of the computers of today. The chip that will be put into your skulls is akin (though far more sophisticated) to those used in those primitive devices." The implanted chip, Mayhar explains, was first used by the military to link field commanders with superiors and computers. Later it was employed by teachers and students, and business managers and technicians. Mayhar writes: "When the interface between the microcomputer and microsurgery was first discovered in the late twenty-first century, there was much concern expressed as to the morality of using such techniques to teach (program) human beings." Eventually the attempt to use the technology with adults failed, and "genetically superior fetuses chosen for creche nurturing were matched via computer and Linked at the age of ten, before being trained for their natural specialties."

While Mayhar's concept of the chip "Links" characters like Andraia and Josip both intellectually and emotionally, she develops alien characters who, in stark contrast, are non-technological and natural empaths. Mayhar also envisions the human tendency to use technology for destructive ends. As Andraia explains to the Deet: "We aren't particularly kind or wise or self-controlled. . . . We think only of ourselves, our interests, our short-term goals. We ruined our own world thousands of years ago. Why should we think we have the right to ruin yours?" Andraia is determined not to allow the peaceful planet of Argent to become another Terran colony, the proving ground for new military technology.

Robotics

Many of those in technology's forefront talk of space colonization as the only hope for the survival of the human race. In most visions of cities in space, robots again play a major role, often scouting new planets, converting (terraforming) them into suitable environments for humans. "These robots would be combination miners, refiners, extruders, and constructors," writes Fjermedal.[4]

Among the novels discussed above, both Forrester and Sargent use robots and AI to support life in space colonies. In *ORVIS*, H. M. Hoover (another of the very fine women writers of science fiction) introduces readers to one of these terraforming robots. ORVIS, an acronym for "Overland Reconnaissance Vehicle in Space," is a "self-educating" robot designed for "early deep space research" who can read, analyze and interpret and has extraordinary cumulative intelligence potential. Robots like ORVIS are considered obsolete and even dangerous; it has been ordered to junk itself at the Corona landfill. However, on its journey to the dump, it meets Toby West, a young girl who doesn't usually like robots. But she finds ORVIS intriguing because it is limping along on six legs and has no face, just a round turret—it looks like a machine. ORVIS is an old model and lacks the android qualities of the newer robots; it even speaks in a machine monotone. Although it is aged and obsolete, it appears to have a sense of self and dignity. While at the Spacer community, ORVIS finds there is little to say to the robotrac planting corn. As the robot travels with Toby and her friend Thaddeus, it begins to wonder about and experience the meaning of the words "care" and "feel." Like many of the scientists working in robotics, Hoover raises questions about robotic life and consciousness.

Are We Alone?

Questions about the development of robotic consciousness are not the only concerns about other life forms in the scientific community. For a long time, humans have wondered about life on other planets and the possibility of contact with alien species. Robert Foward reports in *Future Magic* on the Search for Extra Terrestrial Intelligence (SETI) project, which for some years has been listening for radio signals from the stars.[5] Foward also discusses one scientist's hypothesis regarding the existence of tachyons, particles which (it is theorized) travel faster than the speed of light—and could therefore be used to send messages quickly through space and time. While present theories of physics suggest that tachyons could exist, their actuality has not been proven.

Such a notion is found in *The Stars Will Speak*, in which Lissa has, since the age of ten, been intrigued by the fact that "scientists were listening to signals from an alien civilization somewhere among the stars." She wants to help decipher these signals and has a feeling (as do some scientists today) that the radio signals are not aliens' primary mode of communication, but rather a means of commanding Earth's attention. To achieve her goal, she wishes to attend the Interstellar Institute, a highly selective school established by Adri Shastri, "who first picked up the alien signal in 2064." In what could be a reference to SETI's work, Lissa asks herself, "Why didn't we pick it up in the twentieth century? We were listening." In the 20 years of listening to the signal, Dr. Shastri has been searching for another frequency or more advanced means to decipher it. Lissa suggests tachyons, but realizes they are only hypothetical and have not been proven to exist. Dr. Shastri says that research in tachyons is on the brink of a breakthrough at a listening post on Mars. It is the success of this research that allows the stars to speak. Lissa realizes "tachyon signals [are] hurrying between galactic civilizations, exchanging the only thing in the universe worth trading—information, knowledge, unique viewpoints about the nature of life and the universe."

One important part of the signal is a warning to Earth of the danger of destruction from comets in the Opik-Oort Cloud. Here author Zebrowski refers to Jan Hendrik Oort, a Dutch astronomer who, based on speculations of the astronomer Ernst Opik, "proposed that a vast cloud of unseen comets surrounds the Sun."[6] Zebrowski extrapolates from theories proposed but not proven and provides scenarios which suggest that the future will prove them true.

Fact & Fantasy

Questions concerning the relationship between humans and machines and the role of technology in human life are part of the fact and fiction of contemporary existence. I wholly agree with George Williams, of Harvard University, who says in *The Tomorrow Makers*, "Science fiction is the imagination of society at the edge. It's informed science becoming fantastic and fanciful for the purpose of entertainment, but it might project a future possibility. So I don't think the imagination of science fiction writers is to be discounted."[7] Writers of science fiction for young readers continue to journey to the edge of technology, to create for their readers a future in which the dizzying, as-yet only partially realized scientific developments of our time are fully formed, wondrous and dangerous forces to be reckoned with.

Notes

1. Fjermedal, Grant. *The Tomorrow Makers: A Brave New World of Living-Brain Machines,* Tempus/Microsoft, 1986.

2. Brand, Stewart. *The Media Lab: Inventing the Future at MIT,* Viking, 1987, p. 225.

3. Quoted in Fjermedal, p. 213-14.

4. Fjermedal, p. 254.

5. Forward, Robert L. *Future Magic,* Avon, 1988.

6. Sagan, Carl, and Ann Druyan. *Comet,* Random House, 1985, p. 195.

7. Quoted in Fjermedal, p. 158. ▲

ANNOTATED JOURNAL ARTICLES

Caywood, Carolyn. "The Quest for Character," *School Library Journal* (March 1995): 152.

In fantasy stories the enemies are best cloaked in shadows. The heroes are not always human. The appeal of fantasy is not in denying the complex problems of the real world but in assuring readers that ordinary people can tackle them. The threats confronted in fantasy are very much a part of our own time and fears. Fantasy gives us courage to confront the evils man has created.

Davis, James E., and Alison Smalley. "Attracting Middle-School Readers with William Sleator's *Strange Attractors*," *English Journal* (February 1993): 76-77.

Sleator writes science fiction with elements of realism that keep the stories from becoming too far-fetched. His main characters are contemporary and realistic for the young adult reader. The simplicity of his stories is deceptive. The contemporary ideas and language are what attract readers.

Dowd, Frances A., and Lisa C. Taylor. "Is There a Typical YA Fantasy? A Content Analysis," *Journal of Youth Services in Libraries* (Winter 1992): 175-83.

Fantasy is a paradox: It is literature for escape but it is also a true reflection of reality. Fantasy stimulates the imagination, permits escape while generating hope, and allows a clear vision of values. Fantasy has a great variety of subgenres: mythology, fairy tales, epic sagas, and witchcraft and supernatural. The appeal of this genre is due to its diversity.

Klause, Annette Curtis. "A Hitchhiker's Guide to Science Fiction," *School Library Journal* (September 1988): 120-23.

The golden age for reading science fiction is 12. Science fiction stretches minds by dealing with grand themes that are not hindered by earthly constraints. The greatest theme in science fiction is hope and survival. There is always a future, and the future is ours.

Pierce, Tamora. "Fantasy: Why Kids Read It, Why Kids Need It," *School Library Journal* (October 1993): 50-51.

Even though these stories seem to have little to do with reality, they provoke readers to challenge the status quo. Fantasy opens doors to "What if?" It lets the readers envision other ways of living and thinking. It also creates hope and optimism.

ANNOTATED BIBLIOGRAPHY

Fantasy

Banks, Lynne Reid. *The Magic Hare*. Morrow Junior Books, 1993.

Ten stories about the Magic Hare, who spends his time making a bad-tempered queen pleasant, turning dismal giants into cheerful ones, and ridding the world of horrible dragons. He looks after nameless flowers and frightened orphans and is a delightful character.

Lisle, Janet Taylor. *Afternoon of the Elves*. Orchard, 1989.

The story of strange Sara-Kate Connolly, the neighbor and classmate of Hillary Lennox. Sara-Kate entices Hillary to her overgrown and littered backyard to see the houses made by elves during the night. She tells Hillary all about the elves that live there. Sara-Kate's house is dilapidated, and Hillary never sees Sara-Kate's mother or gets invited in. After Sara-Kate is absent from school for a few days, Hillary goes to see what is wrong and discovers Sara-Kate's secret. The story is sad, and the whole fantasy of the elves gives it a surreal quality.

Wood, Audrey, and Don Wood. *The Tickleoctopus.* Harcourt Brace, 1994.

Ever wonder who was the first person to smile, laugh, and play? Meet Ughpaw, Bub, the caveboy, and Ughmaw. Tickleoctopus is the creature who changed their lives and the history of humanity, as perceived by Audrey and Don Wood.

Science Fiction

Coville, Bruce. *Aliens Ate My Homework.* Pocket Books, 1993.

Rod Allbright is making a volcano for his science project when a spaceship crashes through his bedroom window. The spaceship is disabled and the aliens must stay with Rod until it is fixed. He discovers they are in search of an intergalactic criminal who, it turns out, is someone that Rod knows. When the aliens draft Rod to help them capture the criminal, the excitement really begins.

Wisler, G. Clifton. *The Seer.* Lodestar, 1989.

Scott, an alien from another planet, tries to fit into yet another new school and town. He wears a ring that can take him away from any situation. He can put thoughts into other people's minds and see the future. Scott changes the course of events and then eventually has to leave rather than be found out.

Young, Ruth. *A Trip to Mars.* Orchard, 1990.

A young girl prepares for an imaginary trip to Mars. She thinks of everything—even a space mop, because Mars has dust storms. Two pages of facts about Mars from her space journal are included at the end.

BIBLIOGRAPHY

Fantasy

Adler, C. S. *Good-Bye Pink Pig.* Avon Paper, 1986.

Alexander, Lloyd. *Beggar Queen.* E. P. Dutton, 1984.

———. *The Westmark.* E. P. Dutton, 1981.

Babbitt, Natalie. *The Search for Delicious.* Farrar, Straus & Giroux, 1969.

———. *Tuck Everlasting.* Farrar, Straus & Giroux, 1975.

Boston, L. M. *The Children of the Green Knowe.* Peter Smith, 1989.

Catling, Patrick Skene. *The Chocolate Touch.* Morrow Junior Books, 1979.

Conly, Jane L. *R-T, Margaret, and the Rats of NIMH.* Harper & Row, 1990.

Cooper, Susan. *The Boggart.* Macmillan, 1993.

Coville, Bruce. *Jeremy Thatcher, Dragon Hatcher.* Harcourt Brace Jovanovich, 1991.

Cutler, Margery. *Weird Wolf.* Henry Holt, 1989.

Dadey, Debbie. *Leprechauns Don't Play Basketball.* Scholastic Paper, 1992.

Dahl, Roald. *The BFG.* Farrar, Straus & Giroux, 1982.

———. *James and the Giant Peach.* Alfred A. Knopf, 1961.

Dickinson, Peter. *A Bone from a Dry Sea.* Delacorte Press, 1993.

Eager, Edgar. *Half Magic.* Harcourt Brace Jovanovich, 1954.

Fleischman, Sid. *The Midnight Horse.* Greenwillow Books, 1990.

Fleming, Ian. *Chitty Chitty Bang Bang.* Amereon, 1964.

Gormley, Beatrice. *More Fifth Grade Magic.* Avon Paper, 1990.

Grahame, Kenneth. *The Wind in the Willows.* Macmillan, 1983.

Griffin, Peni R. *Switching Well.* Margaret K. McElderry Books, 1993.

Griffith, Helen V. *Emily and the Enchanted Frog.* Greenwillow Books, 1989.

Hiser, Constance. *No Bean Sprouts, Please!* Holiday House, 1989.

Kleven, Elisa. *The Paper Princess.* Dutton Children's Books, 1994.

Jacques, Brian. *Redwall.* Philomel, 1986.

Jennings, Paul. *Uncanny! Even More Surprising Stories.* Viking, 1991.

Joyce, William. *George Shrinks.* Harper & Row, 1985.

King-Smith, Dick. *Ace: The Very Important Pig.* Crown, 1990.

Le Guin, Ursula K. *Catwings.* Orchard, 1988.

Lewis, C. S. *The Lion, the Witch, and the Wardrobe: A Story for Children.* Macmillan, 1988.

McKinley, Robin. *Beauty.* HarperCollins, 1978.

———. *The Blue Sword.* Greenwillow Books, 1982.

———. *The Hero and the Crown.* Greenwillow Books, 1984.

Norton, Mary. *The Borrowers.* Harcourt Brace Jovanovich, 1953.

O'Brien, Robert. *Mrs. Frisby and the Rats of NIMH.* Macmillan, 1971.

Pierce, Meredith Ann. *Darkangel.* Little, Brown, 1982.

Scieszka, Jon. *Your Mother Was a Neanderthal.* Viking, 1993.

Singer, Marilyn. *California Demon.* Hyperion Books for Children, 1992.

Smith, Sherwood. *Wren's Quest.* Harcourt Brace Jovanovich, 1993.

Snyder, Zilpha Keatley. *Black and Blue Magic.* Atheneum, 1972.

Steig, William. *Abel's Island.* Farrar, Straus & Giroux, 1976.

Stevenson, Jocelyn. *O'Diddy.* Random House, 1988.

Sutcliff, Rosemary. *The Road to Camlann: The Death of King Arthur.* E. P. Dutton, 1982.

Tolkien, J. R. R. *The Hobbit.* Houghton Mifflin, 1938.

Voigt, Cynthia. *The Wings of a Falcon.* Scholastic, 1993.

Wisniewski, David. *Rain Player.* Clarion Books, 1991.

Woodruff, Elvira. *The Summer I Shrank My Grandmother.* Holiday House, 1990.

Science Fiction

Alcock, Vivian. *The Monster Garden.* Doubleday, 1988.

Ames, Mildred. *Anna to the Infinite Power.* Scholastic, 1981.

Byars, Betsy. *The Computer Nut.* Viking Kestrel, 1984.

Cameron, Eleanor. *The Wonderful Flight to the Mushroom Planet.* Little, Brown, 1988.

Christopher, John. *When the Tripods Came.* E. P. Dutton, 1988.

———. *The White Mountains.* Macmillan, 1967.

Danziger, Paula. *This Place Has No Atmosphere.* Delacorte Press, 1986.

de Brunhoff, Laurent. *Babar Visits Another Planet.* Random House, 1972.

DeWeese, Gene. *Black Suits from Outer Space.* Dell, 1985.

Dexter, Catherine. *Mazemaker.* Morrow Junior Books, 1989.

Etra, Jonathan, and Stephanie Spinner. *Aliens for Breakfast.* Random House, 1988.

———. *Aliens for Lunch.* Random House, 1991.

Farmer, Nancy. *The Ear, the Eye, and the Arm.* Orchard, 1994.

Jacobs, Paul Samuel. *Born into Light.* Scholastic, 1988.

Key, Alexander. *Escape to Witch Mountain.* Westminster, 1968.

———. *Flight to the Lonesome Place.* Westminster, 1971.

———. *The Forgotten Door.* Westminster, 1965.

Klause, Annette Curtis. *Alien Secrets.* Delacorte Press, 1993.

Le Guin, Ursula K. *A Wizard of Earthsea.* Houghton Mifflin, 1968.

L'Engle, Madeleine. *A Swiftly Tilting Planet.* Dell, 1978.

———. *A Wind in the Door.* Farrar, Straus & Giroux, 1973.

———. *A Wrinkle in Time.* Farrar, Straus & Giroux, 1962.

Lindbergh, Anne. *The Shadow on the Dial.* Avon Paper, 1988.

Mahy, Margaret. *Aliens in the Family.* Scholastic, 1986.

Norton, Andre. *Voorloper.* Ace Books, 1980.

Park, Ruth. *Playing Beatie Bow.* Atheneum, 1982.

Pinkwater, Daniel Manus. *Guys from Space.* Macmillan, 1989.

———. *Lizard Music.* Dodd, Mead, 1976.

———. *The Snarkout Boys and the Avocado of Death.* Lothrop, Lee & Shepard, 1982.

Roberts, Willo Davis. *The Girl with the Silver Eyes.* Macmillan, 1980.

Sleator, William. *The Boy Who Reversed Himself.* E. P. Dutton, 1986.

———. *Into the Dream.* E. P. Dutton, 1979.

———. *Others See Us.* E. P. Dutton, 1993.

———. *Singularity.* E. P. Dutton, 1985.

———. *Strange Attractors.* E. P. Dutton, 1990.

Walsh, Jill Paton. *The Green Book.* Farrar, Straus & Giroux, 1982.

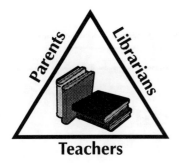

Chapter 9

Nonfiction and Reference

OVERVIEW

Good juvenile nonfiction is direct in its approach to information; it should not detract from naturally dynamic phenomena with condescending discussion. The format should be clear with interesting illustrations. The information should be current, well-organized, and accurate. It should be presented with enthusiasm and cite sources of authority. It should not be distorted or oversimplified.

Nonfiction has always been a popular genre for children. Recently nonfiction for children has mushroomed in both quantity and quality, with titles on every conceivable subject. It is important to encourage children to use reference materials, and there has been a heartening increase in the number and quality of reference books now available.

GUIDED READING QUESTIONS

1. Does the topic interest you? Do you care about it? Is the format attractive? Do the illustrations and information on the first few pages get your attention?

2. Is the information accurate? What is the copyright date? Is it current? Look at the book flap or foreword for the author's credentials: Is he or she qualified to write the book?

3. Are the details consistent? Are the illustrations, charts, and graphs clear? Do they accurately represent the concepts and information presented in the book?

4. Is the information worthwhile? In works of fiction for young children, the author often attributes human traits to animals. This would be questionable in works of nonfiction.

5. Is the text readable? How is the book organized? Is it logical? Does it have a table of contents, index, glossary, and so on?

6. Take a topic you are familiar with and look it up in an encyclopedia and on an electronic encyclopedia. How are they similar? How are they different? Which one covers your topic best? Which do you prefer?

JOURNAL ARTICLE

The News Is Nonfiction

A lively and lucrative field is emerging—one in which
dinosaurs outweigh dragons,
and fantasies give way to the facts.

A good number of books on snakes have appeared recently on publishers' lists: Crowell, Houghton Mifflin, Morrow, Little Simon and—looking a bit into the future—Greenwillow can all boast one or two titles. What are these once unwelcome creatures doing in the well-tended gardens of children's books? Are children being lured more and more toward the realities of the objective world? Are they ready to absorb and enjoy informational books as much as they've enjoyed those about extraterrestrials and enchanted forests? Are the forces of realism gaining momentum in children's books?

It's not just snakes. Dinosaurs, armor, volcanoes and black holes, not to mention rocks, notable people, money and Mars—all these have been prime topics in recent works of nonfiction, with the glossy full-color photographs and expensive reproduction once reserved for adult coffee-table books and big-name artists' picture books. The nonfiction market has changed, and children seem to be both the instigators—indirectly, by their natural curiosity about the world around them—and the beneficiaries of this change.

Not very long ago, nonfiction books were mostly published on a per-curriculum basis: editors acquired works that supplemented or explicated subjects already taught in the classroom. Those books, published for the institutional market, sold well and continue to sell. But nonfiction has especially benefited from the rise of independent children's bookstores. In the meantime, producing full-color photo-essays and nonfiction picture books has become less expensive as publishers have discovered the advantages of printing in the Far East. Parents—dual-income and otherwise—perhaps alarmed by illiteracy rates, have begun to value toys with educational properties, as well as high-quality picture books that offer not only the experience of reading, but convey information as well.

A Picture Book with Punch

Perhaps one of the most popular forms of a nonfiction book is a basic picture book format. *How a Book Is Made* by Aliki (Crowell) is a good starting point; it was aimed at a child's level of interest and understanding, but covered in a fairly comprehensive manner the publishing process.

On the other hand, *Growing Vegetable Soup* by Lois Ehlert is an exemplary book that captures the simple task of making soup from scratch. For Bonnie Ingber, senior editor of Harcourt Brace Jovanovich, acquiring this particular piece of nonfiction was more of a happy accident than a preconceived plan. "I saw [Lois Ehlert's book] on an agent's desk and just had to have

By Kimberly Olson Fakih. Reprinted with permission from *Publishers Weekly* (February 26, 1988), pages 108-11.

it," she says. "It sold out its first printing in two months. And now Lois has a companion volume, *Planting a Rainbow.*"

Then there are the more deliberate attempts to do nonfiction, as in Ann Durell's *Manners That Matter for People Under 21* by Dale Carlson. Formerly publisher of children's books at Dutton, Durell is now editor-at-large for that company. She states, "Several years ago I sensed that kids were really interested in courtesy again." She looked at etiquette books on the market, but was dissatisfied with what she found. "They were mostly done in the '50s—about knives and forks and place settings," she recalls. "But there were traditional things that were still important; I wanted to include those, too."

Some editors' attitudes toward certain nonfiction picture books appropriately match those of kids. From the child's point of view all picture books are reduced to two main categories: interesting and fun or stuffy and boring. All other classifications, like fiction and nonfiction, are irrelevant. Elinor Williams, executive editor at Gulliver Books, who published *New Providence: A Changing Cityscape*, says "This is a personal opinion—I don't have a lot to back it up. But children in the picture book audience don't really know the difference between fiction and nonfiction."

Durell agrees: "Nonfiction today is an exciting mix of the straightforward and the fresh angle; kids don't differentiate between fiction and nonfiction. There is nothing sugarcoated about these books." She points to books such as Roxie Munro's *The Inside-Outside Book of Washington, D.C.* as part of a "new trend with undefinable appeal. And once a book catches on, it's duck soup. It will sell."

Idea and Execution

The editors interviewed invariably restated that the best reason to publish a nonfiction title is that they believe in the book, just as they only acquire fiction titles in which they have a heartfelt interest. Few of them initiate nonfiction ideas or assign them to authors and illustrators; that it's possible to do so remains one of the principal differences between nonfiction and most fiction (although assigning fiction ideas is standard practice among paperback houses and packagers).

Nonfiction usually consists of two main structural parts: an idea and the execution of the idea. Not all concept books are nonfiction, but all nonfiction begins with a concept. Many great ideas, translated into a published work, have proven less than successful. Ideally, there is just as much room for the creativity of the editor as for that of the artist and author. There is the rational approach—Norma Jean Sawicki, marketing director and editor of Orchard Books, is one of those editors who chooses to exercise it: "I have an idea and I try to find someone who is expert or knowledgeable to do it."

Virginia Buckley, editor-in-chief of Lodestar Books, has worked in a similar fashion; she originated the idea for last year's *State Birds*, with Anne Ophelia Dowden in mind as an illustrator for the project. Dowden, in turn, suggested Arthur and Alan Singer, who published two popular field guides and had painted the commemorative stamp block of the birds and flowers of the fifty states for the U.S. Postal Service in 1982. This father-and-son team took on the project, while Buckley provided the text. But that, according to Buckley, was an exception for her. "I never assign ideas," she states. "We may change it, but I prefer to work with what the author knows best."

Durell at Dutton agrees. "For me, nonfiction is almost always generated by the author. I feel that it has to come from inside." She calls the incidents that led to the publication of *Manners That Matter* the exception to the rule.

According to Bernette Ford, publisher at Grossett & Dunlap, there are various ways her imprint acquires nonfiction: co-productions—of which the award-winning *Being Born* was one—and working with packagers; artists bringing ideas to her; and the editorial department generating ideas. "We wanted a series on vehicles," she remembers, "and we had done one in the '60s. But the art was dated, so we're reviving those books with new illustrations."

Ann Troy, senior editor of Clarion Books, generally does not assign ideas. "It's very much the author coming up with the idea. You can put over any idea if someone has written with a lot of passion. We did a first book last fall, *Traveling on an Ocean Liner* by Barbara Haas. She was so enthusiastic, I knew she was going to be good."

Williams at Gulliver notes, "We do a lot of brainstorming in the department to come up with ideas or to find a project for an illustrator we'd like to try." Last year's *New Providence* came about because the Townscape Institute, a group interested in urban renewal, approached the publisher. "Urban renewal was a viable subject for a picture book." Williams says. "Planning groups in cities have used the book, but it's also been used in kindergarten classes."

Nancy Winslow Parker, whose *Bugs* was released by Greenwillow last fall, approached her publisher with the idea—a format that included light verse about bugs as well as scientific diagrams of various species. The fact that she didn't write verse, nor was she an expert in entomology, was a concern for the editors. Elizabeth Shub, senior editor, remembers immediately liking the idea, but with reservations. "Her collaborator [Joan Richards Wright] wrote verse and we told Nancy we had to ensure the accuracy. If you're doing scientific pictures, you have to have them checked by experts."

Shub believes the execution of a good idea to be a difficult task, even for a good writer. "It's very different from fiction. The facts are there, but it's difficult to make them meaningful and exciting for children. The key is to bring the subject into their world."

Durell calls Anne Rockwell a genius for her nonfiction works, which include *How Things Go, Bikes* and this season's *Trains*. "In her books kids can see what's meaningful to them and what's around them," she observes. "Those are picture books, but it's really important to give readers straight information as well."

Trust—And Verify

For some editors, publishing nonfiction means an endless amount of verification and documentation of facts. Troy says, "We screen the writers before we go to contract, and then we rely on their facts. The research is so important—it's a combination of enthusiasm and research skills. Then we try to hire a free-lance copy editor who will check every date and place name, but not do concept research. We don't send out the books to expert readers." Ford at Grossett does send manuscripts and art to experts, but also relies on in-house fact-checking. "We do all the research for the artist, contacting the manufacturers of vehicles and gathering photo materials," she states.

"I would knock a book off the list if it wasn't going to come out accurately," Gulliver's Williams declares. "You trust the author as much as possible but you have to recheck. Even if we don't know something is inaccurate, certainly the readers will."

How can an author make a subject interesting for young readers without sacrificing objectivity in the process? Can footnotes be abolished completely? Or, in cases where information is extracted from another book, can references to page numbers be omitted?

How Is Nonfiction Selling?

At last spring's ABA convention, a special seminar on selling nonfiction in bookstores was well attended. A consensus among booksellers was that up to one-third of their children's book space—whether it was an entire store or one bookshelf—was given over to nonfiction.

Just how well are these books doing? Well, if editors hate to clutter up a nice, readable text with lots of footnotes and graphs, they also hesitate to give away sales figures or the breakdown between institutional and bookstore sales. But here are some numbers on print runs and sales expectations for a selection of titles. These figures only dabble in a subject that is, to say the least, encyclopedic.

Russell Freedman's previous works for Clarion, *Children of the Wild West* and *Cowboys of the Wild West*, each had first-year sales of more than 10,000 copies, later tapering off to approximately 2,500 copies a year. Ann Troy predicted that without the Newbery Medal, *Lincoln* would have sold 15,000-20,000 copies in total, but now it may sell upward of 75,000-80,000 copies. Bernette Ford finds that most of Grossett & Dunlap's print runs for nonfiction hover between 10,000-25,000 copies, but added that *Being Born* sold well above the high end of that estimate (in a reversal of the industry norm, only 10% of most of Grossett's sales are institutional; its market is almost solely in the trade).

New Providence sold over half its first printing of 10,000 copies, and as mentioned, *Growing Vegetable Soup* sold out its first printing entirely.

Chipmunk Song had healthy sales from the beginning, but its sales were given a huge boost when Discovery Toys ordered 40,000 copies for inclusion in its educational toy and game catalogue. For a look at other nonfiction sales, see "The Year of the LRFO" (*PW*, Jan. 23, 1987).

Without such references, the information is likely to be regarded as belonging to the realm of trust, and not, as Troy terms it, "filtered through the author's personality." A reader may not, for example, find the citation for a particular fact and may not know from which of the books in the bibliography that fact was derived. Yet such an omission in a serious work of adult nonfiction would all but ruin the author's credibility.

There are further problems with the bibliography; if the author inadvertently chooses a source that contains misinformation, the errors are perpetuated and become difficult for readers to trace.

Indexes were not always part of nonfiction for young readers, but now few books are published without them. Troy calls documentation "a burning issue among editors—and one that no one is quite certain how to handle. In this kind of book, we're trying to invite children into reading as a pleasurable experience. As an adult, I find it distracting to read footnotes, so I believe it's really asking too much of children of a certain age to go through them." For now, the consensus seems to be that footnotes and extensive chapter notes clutter up an otherwise readable text. (If they are added at all, it is usually at the end.) And that means that making the topic interesting seems to clash with attempts to document the accuracy of the text. The former concern still takes priority over the latter.

Tradition and Novelty

Names such as Jean Fritz, Seymour Simon, Leonard Everett Fisher and Milton Meltzer dominate publishers' offerings of substantial nonfiction, on topics as diverse as *China's Long March* (Fritz), the planets of the solar system (Simon), *The Tower of London* (Fisher) and the lives of the American Revolutionaries, in their own words (Meltzer). These are part of traditional nonfiction publishing, aimed at institutions, but always with a possibility of bookstore sales. Seymour Simon's series on planets has become a bookstore staple, due to the lavishly produced full-color photographs that wouldn't have been possible a few years ago.

Other forms, such as biography, are making more definite headway into the bookstores. Russell Freedman's *Lincoln: A Photobiography*, which was just awarded the Newbery Medal, will strengthen the position of all his books (see last section), published over the years not only by Clarion, but by Holiday House and Dutton as well. Viking Kestrel's Women of Our Time biography series was reprinted in paperback editions on the advice of the company's sales reps. Random House recently reissued 12 books of the Landmark series of historical events, including *Young Mark Twain and the Mississippi, The Landing of the Pilgrims* and *The California Gold Rush*. This season Knopf imported a series called Eyewitness Books, visual catalogues full of objects grouped into specific nonfiction topics: *Arms and Armor* by Michele Byam; *Skeleton* by Steve Parker; *Rocks & Minerals* by the staff of the Natural History Museum, London; and *Bird* by David Burnie. The format, considered "magazine-like" by the publisher, offers readers page after page of glossily photographed objects.

Perhaps the current interest in nonfiction is simply another trend of the moment. It could be that while fiction seems to be ever-moving toward realism, nonfiction is moving toward ever more undefinable formats, such as nonfiction ideas in a fictional format. Somewhere in the middle there are books such as Scholastic's Magic School Bus series by Joanna Cole, illustrated by Bruce Degen, weaving the facts of nonfiction through fictional fabrics. Gail Gibbons has used this format for *The Pottery Place*, Joanne Ryder for *Chipmunk Song* and Marcia Sewall based *The Pilgrims of Plimoth* on actual diary entries by William Bradford and others. Jim Arnosky wrote *Raccoons and Ripe Corn*, while sticking to a more straightforward rendering of his naturalist's viewpoint for *Drawing from Nature* and *Drawing Life in Motion*, among others (*PW*, May 28, 1987).

Emergence of the Photo-Essay

When Patricia Lauber's *Volcano* was awarded a Newbery Honor, it merely confirmed what many people believed all along—that the photo-essay is an art form that is ideal for nonfiction; photography is the highest form of objective representation of reality (after film, of course). Orchard's Norma Jean Sawicki has nurtured this form and, some say, refined it. "If my history is correct, Young Scott Books did a number of photo-essays many years ago," she recalls. "But I never saw them. In terms of contemporary publishing, I think I may have been interested in them before other people." It was during her tenure at Crown that Sawicki first met Lauber; Sawicki edited *Volcano* for Bradbury and also acquired John Chiasson's *African Journey*. She sees hazards in the genre. "People are paying too much attention to the physical beauty of the book and not enough to the text," she says. "I think the serious nonfiction writer is as much of a stylist as a novelist." Noting today's visually oriented society, she believes that whatever the category, "You need a good writer to have a good book—what else is new?"

An engaging text or an interesting idea is still an integral part of any children's book, whether it is a work of fiction or fact presented in an entertaining manner. "We are still finding our way," remarks Clarion's Troy. And there are signs—the awards and increased sales over the last few years—that she and others are succeeding. But the promise is of even more bountiful rewards in the future of nonfiction. ▲

JOURNAL ARTICLE

Frame of Reference

Students need a range of age-appropriate research materials.

I serve as children's librarian for the six locations within my county and as a coordinator of services for the other three counties in our regional system. We have no full-time children's librarian in any of our buildings. For our main library in particular, this has created quite a few problems.

Here, the children's and adult collections are on different floors, so the library is difficult to supervise, especially with our small staff. As a result, the children's area is without supervision most of the time, and students have to go to the adult reference desk upstairs for any assistance.

This created not only an extremely heavy load for the adult reference librarians but also left them constantly trying to find titles that could be used with children. Since I also fill in as an adult reference librarian, I was doubly aware of the problems. This experience has really helped

By Barbara J. Walker. Reprinted with permission from *School Library Journal* (October 1994), page 56. Barbara J. Walker is the Aiken County Children's Librarian at the Aiken-Bamberg-Barnwell-Edgefield Regional Library System in Aiken, SC.

me see the need for better reference materials in children's departments. I don't think many of us have recognized how important it is to build up this area of our collection.

If you visit the reference shelves in most children's departments you will find the same basic sources. There will be one or more sets of general encyclopedias, an atlas or two, a couple of dictionaries, science encyclopedias—these we deem essential to meet the requirements of report writers. Yet, every librarian knows that most children will have to reach beyond these resources. So we scramble all over the adult reference collection trying to find something that children can comprehend to answer their questions.

In recent months, for example, several classes had been assigned to write papers on famous people in science and mathematics. Most of these required students to use five to ten sources in their research. Many of the sources found carried only a brief biographical sketch. Scribner's *Dictionary of Scientific Biography* often carried quite an extensive amount of information but was much too advanced for some of the students. We could see the look of dread on their faces when they opened the book. Some of them were too embarrassed to say they didn't understand what had been placed before them, so they simply took the book back to their table and continued to look for other materials on their own. Some tried to scan through and pick out what they could, while others simply gave up. With some sources, we had to virtually interpret the written material as the student took notes from our explanation. At any rate the need for information was not being met. The goal of getting students to read and interpret for themselves, however, can be accomplished with only limited assistance when the materials are geared to the appropriate age or grade.

With the budget crunch on everywhere, I realize that most of us can't spend a lot of money on individual juvenile reference books. We can, however, plan to purchase at least one children's reference title from time to time. The use will warrant the expense. We know, for example, that our library will be hit every year with state reports that require pictures, so we ordered the books *State Birds, State Flags, State Flowers,* and *State Trees* (1992, all Watts) for our reference collection. We now have a ready source with a picture and some brief information on each state. Another way around a tight budget is to consider whether some of your often circulated nonfiction titles would better serve on the reference shelf.

A solid juvenile reference collection can also serve a broad range of library customers. There are occasions when the adult reference sources are inappropriate for some older students or adults with lower reading skills, occasions when a children's reference book will be the perfect resource. Also, most librarians who work with children's sources know that, regardless of the education level of the customer, the best way to become familiar with any new area of study is to first approach it through the juvenile collection. There a reader can gain a basic understanding of the topic before moving on to more advanced sources in the adult collection.

Juvenile reference books also can be an asset in drawing gift support. Most of the gift money given for children's materials will be spent on picture books, which will carry a bookplate bearing the donor's name. Many people look for their names in new books (if they have given specifically for that purpose), and if they don't see it, may inquire about the funds given. (It rarely seems to occur to them that the books have been checked out.) We now try to purchase at least one children's reference title with each sizable gift. This way there will always be at least one book available with that person or group's bookplate. This allows us to slowly build a specialized reference collection while at the same time giving donors a chance to see something on the shelves that was purchased with their gift.

But, the best reason for building a broad collection of children's reference materials is because it will more easily allow students to do research on their own. This greater independence will enable them to get a stronger grasp on the subject they're studying and help them to become better students. Once they become aware of the resources available to them in juvenile reference, they will begin to use that collection more frequently, relieving the burden on adult reference librarians who are more familiar with adult resources and not as equipped to meet the needs of younger researchers. ▲

ANNOTATED JOURNAL ARTICLES

Carter, Betty, and Richard F. Abrahamson. "The Role of Nonfiction in the Development of Lifetime Readers," *Journal of Youth Services in Libraries* (Summer 1991): 363-68.

The increasing interest in children's nonfiction now accounts for 50 to 85 percent of total juvenile circulation in school and public libraries. The authors explain the five stages of reading development, indicating how readers pass from one stage to another. Nonfiction plays an important part in the development of lifetime readers.

Kister, Ken. "Multimedia Encyclopedias Take Off," *Wilson Library Bulletin* (May 1995): 42-45.

Changes in encyclopedias have occurred at warp speed, with students, parents, teachers, and school librarians finding these changes very appealing. Never before have students come into the library so eager to use encyclopedias! These CD-ROM versions are examples of multimedia in the early stages; reference librarians of the next century face choices we cannot begin to imagine.

Snowball, Diane. "Building Literacy Skills Through Nonfiction," *Teaching K-8* (May 1995): 62-63.

Students who struggle with writing may be more interested in doing research about a topic that interests them and writing a nonfiction piece. Therefore, students need to know how to read nonfiction to get the information they want and then how to organize the information and write a complete presentation.

SUGGESTED STUDENT'S HOME REFERENCE COLLECTION

Encyclopedia (electronic or print version)
Dictionary
Thesaurus
Atlas
Almanac
Foreign-language dictionaries (if languages are being studied)

ANNOTATED BIBLIOGRAPHY

Bial, Raymond. *The Underground Railroad.* Houghton Mifflin, 1995.

Every page has a photograph that depicts the Underground Railroad or the slave conditions that led to its establishment. The Underground Railroad was an informal network of routes that led to the northern states and free Canada. This "railroad" was most active in the 60 years before the Civil War. Tens of thousands of slaves escaped by way of the Underground Railroad. A chronology of the antislavery movement in America appears at the end of the book. The theme of the book is best stated in its text: "[T]he worst of times always brings out the very best in some people," and such is the story of the Underground Railroad.

Eyewitness Visual Dictionary of Plants. Dorling Kindersley, 1992.

There are more than 300,000 species of plants. The most numerous are the flowering plants, with 250,000 species. This visual dictionary explores plants both inside and out. Dryland plants, wetland plants, carnivorous plants, epiphytic (air), and parasitic plants are displayed with short text and numerous illustrations. Some of the other titles in this series include ships and sailing, the human body, animals, cars, and military uniforms.

Kendall, Russ. *Russian Girl: Life in an Old Russian Town*. Scholastic, 1994.

Olga Surikova is nine years old and going into the third grade. She lives in Suzdal, a small Russian town, 150 miles east of Moscow. Photographs give the reader an insight into Olga's daily routine of school and home life. This photodocumentary gives children a better understanding of a culture different from their own.

Pringle, Laurence. *Scorpion Man: Exploring the World of Scorpions*. Charles Scribner's Sons, 1994.

During his graduate schooling, Gary Polis realized that little was known about scorpions. In the early 1970s, armed with an ultraviolet lamp, Gary drove to the desert to find and study scorpions, which glow under ultraviolet light. Scorpions live in many habitats: deserts, jungles, grasslands, caves, seashores, and high in mountains. The lack of activity of these ancient animals helps them survive. They can live without food for a year and may live as long as 25 years. Only 25 of the 1,500 known species have enough venom to kill a person. These arachnids are fascinating to study as well as valuable in drug development and neurological research.

Rogozinski, Jan. *Pirates! Brigands, Buccaneers, and Privateers in Fact, Fiction, and Legend*. Facts on File, 1995.

This comprehensive, A-to-Z encyclopedia includes all pirates, both fictional and real, who affected the course of human history. It also includes accessible works of fiction and all English-language movies with a piratical theme. Many of the photographs are from famous pirate movies and works of art. It includes cross-references, a selective bibliography, and an index.

Van Rose, Susanna. *The Earth Atlas*. Dorling Kindersley, 1994.

Earth is 4.5 billion years old. The forces that shaped and changed its surface and the variety of landscapes that resulted are explained through text, maps, photographs, and diagrams. This is an exciting new visual guide to our unique planet.

BIBLIOGRAPHY

Alexander, Sally Hobart. *Mom Can't See Me*. Macmillan, 1990.

Aliki. *Digging Up Dinosaurs*. Thomas Y. Crowell, 1988.

———. *The Gods and Goddesses of Olympus*. HarperCollins, 1994.

Ames, Lee J. *Draw 50 Sharks, Whales, and Other Sea Creatures*. Doubleday, 1989.

Anderson, William. *Laura Ingalls Wilder Country*. HarperPerennial, 1990.

Anno, Mitsumasa. *Anno's Medieval World*. Philomel, 1979.

Appalachia: The Voices of Sleeping Birds. Harcourt Brace Jovanovich, 1991.

Ardely, Neil. *Music: An Illustrated Encyclopedia*. Facts on File, 1986.

Arnold, Caroline. *Elephant*. Morrow Junior Books, 1993.

Boughton, Simon. *Great Lives*. Doubleday, 1988.

Brighton, Catherine. *Mozart: Scenes from the Childhood of the Great Composer*. Doubleday, 1990.

Carr, Terry. *Spill! The Story of the Exxon Valdez*. Franklin Watts, 1991.

Cherry, Lynne. *A River Ran Wild*. Harcourt Brace Jovanovich, 1992.

Cohen, Daniel. *Great Ghosts*. Dutton Children's Books, 1990.

Dixon, Dougal. *Dougal Dixon's Dinosaurs*. Boyds Mills Press, 1993.

Early, Margaret. *William Tell*. Harry N. Abrams, 1991.

Evslin, Bernard. *The Family Read-Aloud Holiday Treasury*. Little, Brown, 1991.

——. *The Sphinx*. Chelsea House, 1991.

Feldman, Eve B. *Animals Don't Wear Pajamas*. Henry Holt, 1992.

Few, Roger. *Macmillan Children's Guide to Endangered Animals*. Macmillan, 1993.

Freedman, Russell. *The Wright Brothers*. Holiday House, 1991.

Geras, Adele. *My Grandmother's Stories: A Collection of Jewish Folk Tales*. Alfred A. Knopf, 1990.

Gibbons, Gail. *A Book About Signals*. Morrow Junior Books, 1993.

——. *The Puffins Are Back*. HarperCollins, 1991.

Gonen, Rivka. *Charge! Weapons and Warfare in Ancient Times*. Runestone Press, 1993.

Graymount, Barbara. *The Iroquois*. Chelsea House, 1988.

Gustafson, Anita. *Some Feet Have Noses*. Lothrop, Lee & Shepard, 1983.

Haldane, Suzanne. *Helping Hands*. Dutton Children's Books, 1991.

Hamilton, Virginia. *The Dark Way: Stories from the Spirit World*. Harcourt Brace Jovanovich, 1990.

——. *The People Could Fly: American Black Folktales*. Alfred A. Knopf, 1985.

Harness, Cheryl. *Young John Quincy*. Bradbury Press, 1994.

Jacobs, William Jay. *Lincoln*. Charles Scribner's Sons, 1991.

Jones, Charlotte Foltz. *Mistakes That Worked*. Doubleday, 1991.

Kuklin, Susan. *Going to My Gymnastics Class*. Bradbury Press, 1991.

——. *Thinking Big: The Story of a Young Dwarf*. Lothrop, Lee & Shepard, 1986.

Lampton, Christopher. *Earthquake*. Millbrook Press, 1991.

Landau, Elaine. *Dyslexia*. Franklin Watts, 1991.

Lauber, Patricia. *Dinosaurs Walked Here*. Bradbury Press, 1987.

——. *From Flower to Flower: Animals and Pollination*. Crown, 1986.

——. *Seeing Earth from Space*. Orchard, 1990.

Lester, Julius. *To Be a Slave*. Dial Press, 1968.

Madison, Arnold. *Drugs and You*. Julian Messner, 1990.

Maestro, Betsy. *The Story of Money*. Clarion Books, 1993.

Maestro, Betsy, and Giulio Maestro. *The Discovery of the Americas*. Lothrop, Lee & Shepard Books, 1991.

McGuire, Kevin. *Woodworking for Kids*. Sterling, 1993.

McKissack, Patricia, and Frederick McKissack. *Christmas in the Big House, Christmas in the Quarters*. Scholastic, 1994.

McWhirter, Norris. *Guinness Sports Record Book*. Sterling, 1986.

Meltzer, Milton. *Gold*. HarperCollins, 1993.

Mott, Evelyn Clarke. *Steam Train Ride*. Walker, 1991.

Murphy, Jim. *The Boys War.* Clarion Books, 1990.

Osborne, Mary Pope. *American Tall Tales.* Alfred A. Knopf, 1991.

Parker, Nancy Winslow. *Bugs.* Greenwillow Books, 1987.

Patent, Dorothy Hinshaw. *Gray Wolf, Red Wolf.* Clarion Books, 1990.

———. *Pelicans.* Clarion Books, 1992.

Penner, Lucille Recht. *Eating the Plates: A Pilgrim Book of Food and Manners.* Macmillan, 1991.

Petersen-Fleming, Judy. *Kitten Care and Critters, Too!* Tambourine Books, 1994.

Pringle, Laurence. *Oil Spills: Damage, Recovery and Prevention.* Morrow Junior Books, 1993.

Raboff, Ernest. *Henri Rousseau.* J. B. Lippincott, 1988.

Rankin, Laura. *The Handmade Alphabet.* Dial Books for Young Readers, 1991.

Rogasky, Barbara. *Smoke and Ashes: The Story of the Holocaust.* Holiday House, 1988.

Ryden, Hope. *Joey: The Story of a Baby Kangaroo.* Tambourine Books, 1994.

Sargent, William. *Night Reef.* Franklin Watts, 1991.

Schnieper, Claudia. *Amazing Spiders.* Carolrhoda Books, 1989.

Schwartz, Alvin. *Cross Your Fingers, Spit in Your Hat.* J. B. Lippincott, 1974.

———. *Gold & Silver, Silver & Gold: Tales of Hidden Treasure.* Farrar, Straus & Giroux, 1988.

Seymour, John. *The Forgotten Household Crafts.* Alfred A. Knopf, 1987.

Siebert, Diane. *Plane Song.* HarperCollins, 1993.

Simon, Seymour. *Our Solar System.* Morrow Junior Books, 1992.

Stanley, Diane. *Charles Dickens.* Morrow Junior Books, 1993.

Stanley, Jerry. *Children of the Dust Bowl: The True Story of the School at Weedpatch Camp.* Crown, 1992.

Steele, Phillip. *Sharks and Other Creatures of the Deep.* Dorling Kindersley, 1991.

Taylor, Barbara. *Shoreline.* Dorling Kindersley, 1993.

Terban, Marvin. *Hey, Hay! A Wagonful of Funny Homonym Riddles.* Clarion Books, 1991.

———. *Mad as a Wet Hen! And Other Funny Idioms.* Clarion Books, 1987.

Verdy, Violette. *O Swans, Sugarplums and Satin Slippers: Ballet Stories for Children.* Scholastic, 1991.

Walker, Barbara M. *The Little House Cookbook.* Harper & Row, 1979.

Wheatley, George. *The Young Rider's Companion.* Lerner, 1981.

White, Sandra Verrill. *Sterling: The Rescue of a Baby Harbor Seal.* Crown, 1989.

Wilkes, Angela. *My First Nature Book.* Alfred A. Knopf, 1990.

Willard, Nancy. *Beauty and the Beast.* Harcourt Brace Jovanovich, 1992.

Wulffson, Don L. *Incredible True Adventures.* Dodd, Mead, 1986.

Young, Ruth. *Starring Francine & Dave: Three One-Act Plays.* Orchard, 1988.

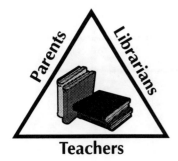

Parents Librarians Teachers

Chapter 10

Bibliotherapy or Problem Novels

OVERVIEW

Bibliotherapy is the use of reading material to help solve emotional problems and promote mental health. If children who are having problems can read about others who have encountered and solved comparable dilemmas, they may see hope for themselves. From their reading, children can see that they are not alone with apprehension, anxiety, and disappointment. Literature can illuminate situations so that children can empathize with friends, classmates, or family members with similar problems. Through fictional characters, children can experience different situations and share feelings. They can also become more aware of human motivation and so understand their own behaviors and feelings. Books tend to carry a special kind of authority with children. Those who doubt adults or peers may be more trusting of books. In that case, books may be valuable companions for the developing child.

GUIDED READING QUESTIONS

1. What is the problem in your book? Is the problem overwhelming? Are the character(s) trapped and helpless?

2. Are the character(s) able to solve their own problems in a satisfactory manner and maintain hope?

3. What do you like about the main character(s)?

4. Are you able to identify with the feelings, actions, or goals of the main character?

5. Are the adults in your book portrayed as strong, helpful, and sensitive, or are they weak and insensitive?

6. As you read your book, did you encounter any thoughts, feelings, or actions that could be applied to your life?

7. Would you recommend this book to be used with a group of students for reading and discussion?

From *The Reading Connection.* © 1997. Libraries Unlimited. (800) 237-6124.

JOURNAL ARTICLE

In Defense of Fun

. . . the two-parent, reasonably happy, supportive family is practically nonexistent in today's literature for children.

In 1992 I had the privilege of serving on the Newbery Committee. While reading an average of ten books a week for that group and reading various other books besides, I discovered some interesting trivia. For example, one week I read three books set in west Texas: *Oh, Those Harper Girls* (Kathleen Karr, Farrar, 1992), *Hobkin* (Peni Griffey, McElderry, 1992), and *Jo and the Bandit* (Willo Davis Roberts, Atheneum, 1992). One can only conclude that somewhere in west Texas about three years ago there was one fantastic authors conference. Then, when reading the nominees for the 1993/94 Mark Twain Book Award, I noticed that a few of the books mentioned washcloths: Two were colored yellow—the third washcloth was blue.

While discovering or recognizing trivial coincidences was fun, I also had time to reflect on some less trivial commonalities. For example, of the twenty 1993/94 Mark Twain Book Award nominees, five dealt with abandoned children, five were dog stories, and two children and a dog die. Also my intensive reading leads me to believe that

By Anitra T. Steele and Kathleen T. Horning. Reprinted with permission from *Wilson Library Bulletin* (December 1993), pages 57-59. Anitra T. Steele is Children's Specialist, Mid-Continent Public Library, Independence, Missouri. Kathleen T. Horning is a half-time Librarian at both the Madison (Wisconsin) Public Library and the Cooperative Children's Book Center. The pair collaborate and alternate writing this column.

the two-parent, reasonably happy, supportive family is practically nonexistent in today's literature for children.

In thinking over the books I read in 1992, only two such families come to mind—the Preston family in *Shiloh* (Phyllis Reynolds Naylor, Atheneum, 1991) and Morning Girl and Star Boy's family in *Morning Girl* (Michael Dorris, Hyperion, 1992). This family of Taino Indians would be hard for today's child to emulate. You might respond that now, many children come from nontraditional families; that these books show children developing for themselves the support network they need, as in Jane Cutler's *Family Dinner* (Farrar, 1992). While that criticism is true, does literature always have to imitate life so closely? One of the reasons children enjoy reading is for escape, and a story about a supportive and loving family could be escapist literature for those children who never see one—except on reruns of *Leave It to Beaver*.

While I was reading last year, I shared many of the books with my two children, then ages eleven and twelve. The twelve-year-old read widely, accepting suggestions and giving feedback. The eleven-year-old was more likely to read only a few pages and return the book to me for something with more adventure. When questioned closely, he explained that he didn't want any books about problems, he just wanted books about kids doing fun things. If I didn't have that, something about fish or amphibians would do. In fact, his recommendation for the Newbery Medal was a title from a small press, *Jasper and Sam: A Story of Friendship and Adventure* (David Reichley, Evanston Publishing, 1992). He read this book, a story set in the 1950s about a prankish boy with a strong conscience, several times, and uses it for comparison even now.

Bibliotherapy vs. Pleasure

Are children's authors and children's librarians trying too hard? Does every book have to address some problem children may experience, merely to justify its existence? Yes, babies have been accidently or even purposely switched in hospitals, but do children need *Sharing Susan* (Eve Bunting, HarperCollins, 1991) to make them feel insecure about their place in their families, especially if they don't look like their parents?

Bibliotherapy has its place and performs a valid function in today's society, but recently every book seems to be therapeutic. And if it is therapeutic, is it giving the message we want to disseminate?

In the five books about abandoned children mentioned earlier, while Family Services eventually enters most of the stories, reliance on this system or even a willingness to use this social safety net is portrayed as an alternative worse than going it alone and living on the streets. Family Services and its attendant bureaucracy is not an enticing choice for children, but by bad-mouthing it so consistently in children's books (one exception, *Tough Chauncy* [Doris Buchanan Smith, Puffin, 1986]) it ceases to become a viable option for children who may need it.

I am not promulgating a return to banal Pollyannaish literature for children. I realize that in books about abandoned children, if they were immediately taken up by social workers, there would be no story. In the books where Family Services did finally intercede, there was appreciative acknowledgment by the characters. Nevertheless, there seems to be a surfeit of those kinds of stories lately.

There were some very thought-provoking and personally enlightening stories in 1992. *If Rock and Roll Were a Machine* (Terry Davis, Delacorte, 1992) depicts what can happen to a child when a teacher singles him out for long-term ridicule. Many readers can probably identify rightly or wrongly with Bert Bowden. Dealing with an aberrant personality is portrayed in *Breaking the Fall* (Michael Cadnum, Viking, 1992). The snakelike fascination of a psychotic personality is clearly shown—thought-provoking and chilling.

Becoming Adults

Dealing with growing up, always a popular theme, got some new wrinkles in 1992. A minor theme in *The Friendship Song* (Nancy Springer, Atheneum, 1992) covers in-school sexual harassment. Having been in junior high in the sixties, I hadn't given much thought to that as a problem. However, after reading about it in *The Friendship Song* and seeing several newspaper articles about sexual harassment in schools, I talked with my daughter, a middle school student, and informed her if someone tries to touch her at school, she has my permission to deck him. I'll serve detention with her if need be.

The truth has also wrinkled the growing up theme. In both *Liars* (P. J. Petersen, Simon & Schuster, 1992) and *Eye of the Beholder* (Daniel Hayes, Godine, 1992) young people who know the truth have a hard time dealing with the adults around them. In *Liars*, Sam suddenly develops the ability to tell if another person is lying. This is frightening for the rural Oregon eighth grader, especially when he finds his father constantly lying to him about things that shouldn't matter. As a prank in *Eye of the Beholder,* Tyler and Lymie create a couple of stone heads in the style of an artist who once lived in their town, only to discover with horror that the town's "artistic" leaders believe the heads were the work of the artist. Getting the grown-ups to see the truth is a lot harder than one might believe.

The correct handling of truth (not just in the superfluous, "politically correct" sense) in children's books is like the treatment of child abandonment or abuse, another sensitive issue. Authors need to consider the underlying message they are giving by their characters' reactions to lies and the consequences for characters of falsehoods. In *Liars,* Sam interprets his father's lies as a lack of trust, something that by the end of the novel is cleared up. Tyler and Lymie, on the other hand, end up in hot water, albeit not too hot, for their prank, even though it only made the adults look foolish.

The Danger of Dilution

Being topical has found its way into all kinds of children's books. The Berenstain Bears teach stranger danger as well as the trauma of too much birthday. Babysitters Club members must cope with blended families, and all is not just young love for the students of Sweet Valley High. Part of me applauds this trend. After all, the more kids understand about the seriousness of drinking and driving or getting into a stranger's car, the safer they will be. Another part of me worries, though, about diluting the impact of the message with broadcast repetition. Will important lessons become like Marcus Welby's "disease of the week" or in the vernacular of *Liars'* Marty McNabb, "SOT" and "MOSOT" ("Same Old Thing" and "More Of the Same Old Thing")?

After several years of apron counting in the seventies, interest in sexism in children's books died away. This year, there does seem to be lots of good, strong female characters in children's books: look at Mirette (Emily Arnold McCully, *Mirette on the High Wire,* Putnam, 1992) and Summer (Cynthia Rylant, *Missing May,* Orchard, 1992). Now that the apron counters have left the scene, it appears they took the apron wearers with them.

Ageism would probably have suffered the same fate had it not been for author/illustrator James Stevenson. His Grandpa books and others he has illustrated, like *Loop the Loop* (Barbara Dugan, Greenwillow, 1992), have almost single-handedly kept alive the idea of sprightly elders interacting with youngsters for their mutual benefit. Sensitivity is so much preferable to nonentity.

One small exception to this embracing of topicality is the number of fine autobiographies being published for children by children's book authors. *Moon and I* (Betsy Byars, Messner, 1992) is a wonderful example of a fun reading story (with snakes!) that can be simply enjoyed.

The bean counters tell us that more children's books are being published than ever before. Children reading today have a wider and more varied field to select from. If that is true, couldn't some authors go back to the old-fashioned adventure story and not make topical, typical? Can't reading be simply fun? ▲

ANNOTATED JOURNAL ARTICLES

Caywood, Carolyn. "Risky Business," *School Library Journal* (May 1995): 44.

Adolescence must be a time of risk-taking, or teens would never leave home and become independent. Stories can help teens take those initial steps by showing that they can be independent without forfeiting friends. The author lists titles of books showing that teens can be somebody without succumbing to peer pressure.

Gubert, Betty K. "Sadie Peterson Delaney: Pioneer Bibliotherapist," *American Libraries* (February 1993): 124-29.

Delaney was a librarian who provided library service to thousands of physically and mentally disabled African American veterans. She had a knack for the art of bibliotherapy and received worldwide recognition. She spent a lot of time reading books so that she could recommend just the right book to the right patient. She sought to reduce internal anxieties and aggressions, to alleviate boredom, and to promote the patients' personal growth through bibliotherapy.

Hendrickson, Linda B. "The 'Right' Book for the Child in Distress," *School Library Journal* (April 1988): 40-41.

The author describes bibliotherapy as finding the right book for the right child. Bibliotherapy is a valid and reasonable way of helping children cope with emotional disruptions they encounter. Current books cover a wide variety of topics, so it is important to select just the right book to help a child with a problem. Bibliotherapy can be a classroom activity, to allow divergent thinking and discussions among students. Discussions after the book is read are extremely important.

Nilsen, Alleen Pace. "That Was Then . . . This Is Now," *School Library Journal* (April 1994): 30-33.

The author points out that many young adults watch the afternoon talk shows. Problem novels about whether Susie will get a date for the prom seem to pale in comparison to the topics on the standard talk shows. We live in a climate of true confession with these shows. The glut of unusual topics being explored leaves little subject matter for current authors. The author predicts fewer problem novels will be written in the future and more and more youth-oriented problems will be aired on talk shows. She claims that there is still a strong need for well-written books to counterbalance the media treatment of problems.

Steele, Anitra T. "Read Two Books and Call Me in the Morning," *Wilson Library Bulletin* (June 1994): 65-66.

Many small incidences of stress and "disaster" affect children without adults even being aware of the trauma caused. Librarians always seem to tell cautionary tales at story time to help prepare children for the effects of problems and stress. It is important for children to have access to the right books at just the right time.

ANNOTATED BIBLIOGRAPHY

Danziger, Paula. *Amber Brown Is Not a Crayon*. Scholastic, 1994.

Amber Brown's parents are divorced, so she knows what it feels like to miss someone. She learns that her best friend, Justin, is moving away. Amber picks a fight with Justin so it won't seem so hard when he moves. They resolve their fight, to the relief of all who know them. After Justin moves, whenever Amber thinks about third grade, she thinks of Justin.

Duffey, Betsy. *The Math Wiz*. Viking, 1990.

Marty Malone, the math wiz, starts third grade in a new school. Marty always thought there was no problem too big for him to solve. That was before Coach McMillian called "choosing teams." Marty is always chosen last. He is the worst kid in P.E. He thinks of his P.E. problem like this:

Math Wiz + P.E. = Misery

The solution to his problem becomes:

Math Wiz + P.E. + A Friend = All Right!!!

MacLachlan, Patricia. *Journey*. Delacorte Press, 1991.

Journey's mother left him and his sister, Cat, with their grandparents when Journey was 11. Everyone except Journey seemed to know that his mother wouldn't be back. Like his grandfather, Journey develops a keen interest in photography. He searches old photos for clues and information about his mother. In time, Journey learns to accept the past as well as the present.

Rabe, Berniece. *Margaret Moves*. E. P. Dutton, 1987.

Margaret sees a sports-model wheelchair at a special basketball game for handicapped players. How can she convince her parents that she needs such an expensive chair as well as a canopy bed? Margaret tries to accomplish her dreams through many money-making schemes. One special weekend the salesman lets her try the new wheelchair. At last, she experiences speed. Margaret has her ups and downs, but she keeps her own spirits up along with the reader's.

Roberts, Willo Davis. *What Are We Going to Do About David?* Atheneum, 1993.

In the middle of the night, David hears his parents fighting. He hears them say, "What are we going to do with David?" It is as if he is a dog and they have to decide on a boarding kennel. David is left with his grandmother, Ruthie, and Susie, her dog. Ruthie lives on her meager savings in a small coastal Washington town. David misses his parents more than they seem to miss him. Even after a month, his parents don't know if they want him or each other. David finally opens up and says he wants to stay with Ruthie and Susie. For the first time in a long while, he feels cared for and at home.

Smith, Doris Buchanan. *The Pennywhistle Tree*. Putnam, 1991.

They know the neighborhood will not be the same when the George family unpacks the yellow school bus. Jonathan and his friends watch from their tree. Children are everywhere, seven of them. Jonathan reluctantly starts being nice to the eldest child, Sanders. Does he have to give up his old friends to be kind to someone they don't like? Does being kind to Sanders mean that he is stuck with Sanders as a friend for life? Just when Jonathan begins to understand his relationship with Sanders, everything changes.

BIBLIOGRAPHY

Family Relationships

Alcott, Louisa May. *Little Women*. Putnam, 1947.

Bauer, Marion Dane. *On My Honor*. Houghton Mifflin, 1986.

Blume, Judy. *It's Not the End of the World*. Macmillan, 1982.

Bunting, Eve. *Fly Away Home*. Clarion Books, 1992.

———. *Sharing Susan*. HarperCollins, 1991.

Burch, Robert. *Ida Early Comes over the Mountain.* Viking, 1980.

Byars, Betsy. *The Blossoms Meet the Vulture Lady.* Delacorte Press, 1986.

Cameron, Ann. *The Stories Julian Tells.* Pantheon, 1981.

Cleary, Beverly. *Ramona, Forever.* William Morrow, 1984.

———. *Socks.* William Morrow, 1973.

Cleaver, Vera, and Bill Cleaver. *Where the Lilies Bloom.* New American Library, 1969.

Delton, Judy. *Angel's Mother's Boyfriend.* Houghton Mifflin, 1986.

Estes, Eleanor. *The Moffats.* Scholastic, 1941.

Hamilton, Virginia. *M. C. Higgins the Great.* Macmillan, 1974.

Hurwitz, Johanna. *Russell and Elisa.* Morrow Junior Books, 1989.

Jukes, Mavis. *Like Jake and Me.* Alfred A. Knopf, 1984.

Lasky, Kathryn. *The Night Journey.* Puffin Books, 1981.

Locker, Thomas. *Family Farm.* Dial Books for Young Readers, 1988.

McCully, Emily Arnold. *Picnic.* Harper & Row, 1984.

McKenna, Colleen O'Shaughnessy. *Too Many Murphys.* Scholastic, 1988.

Naylor, Phyllis Reynolds, and Lura Schield Reynolds. *Maudie in the Middle.* Macmillan, 1988.

Paterson, Katherine. *Jacob Have I Loved.* Thomas Y. Crowell, 1980.

———. *Park's Quest.* Thomas Y. Crowell, 1988.

Rylant, Cynthia. *When I Was Young in the Mountains.* E. P. Dutton, 1982.

Smith, Janice Lee. *The Monster in the Third Dresser Drawer and Other Stories About Adam Joshua.* Harper & Row, 1981.

Smith, Robert K. *The War with Granpa.* Dell, 1984.

Spyri, Johanna. *Heidi.* Putnam, 1945.

Taylor, Mildred D. *Roll of Thunder, Hear My Cry.* Bantam Books, 1976.

Taylor, Sydney. *All-of-a-Kind Family.* Peter Smith, 1980.

Voigt, Cynthia. *Dicey's Song.* Atheneum, 1982.

Wallace, Bill. *Beauty.* Holiday House, 1988.

Wilder, Laura Ingalls. *Little House in the Big Woods.* Harper & Row, 1953.

Understanding Personal Problems

Bauer, Marion Dane. *Rain of Fire.* Houghton Mifflin, 1983.

Blume, Judy. *Blubber.* Macmillan, 1982.

———. *Otherwise Known as Sheila the Great.* E. P. Dutton, 1972.

Brown, Marc. *Arthur's Nose.* Little, Brown, 1986.

Cleary, Beverly. *Dear Mr. Henshaw.* William Morrow, 1983.

———. *Strider.* William Morrow, 1991.

Conly, Jane L. *Crazy Lady!* HarperCollins, 1993.

Conrad, Pam. *Prairie Songs.* Harper & Row, 1985.

———. *Staying Nine.* Harper & Row, 1988.

DeClements, Barthe. *Five-Finger Discount.* Delacorte Press, 1989.

dePaola, Tomie. *Oliver Button Is a Sissy.* Harcourt Brace Jovanovich, 1979.

Giff, Patricia Reilly. *Matthew Jackson Meets the Wall.* Delacorte Press, 1990.

Haugen, Tormod. *The Night Birds.* Delacorte Press, 1982.

Herzig, Alison C., and Jane L. Mali. *Sam and the Moon Queen.* Houghton Mifflin, 1980.

Hurwitz, Johanna. *Once I Was a Plum Tree.* William Morrow, 1980.

Jossee, Barbara M. *Anna, the One and Only.* J. B. Lippincott, 1988.

Jukes, Mavis. *Blackberries in the Dark.* Alfred A. Knopf, 1993.

Kinsey-Warnock, Natalie. *The Canada Geese Quilt.* Cobblehill, 1989.

Klass, Sheila. *Kool Ada.* Scholastic, 1991.

Levy, Elizabeth. *Lizzie Lies a Lot.* Delacorte Press, 1976.

Manes, Stephen. *Be a Perfect Person in Just Three Days.* Clarion Books, 1982.

Miles, Betty. *The Trouble with Thirteen.* Alfred A. Knopf, 1979.

Mills, Lauren. *The Rag Coat.* Little, Brown, 1991.

Montgomery, L. M. *Anne of Green Gables.* Bantam Books, 1987.

Namioka, Lensey. *Yang the Youngest and His Terrible Ear.* Little, Brown, 1992.

Paterson, Katherine. *The Great Gilly Hopkins.* Thomas Y. Crowell, 1978.

Patron, Susan. *Maybe Yes, Maybe No, Maybe Maybe.* Orchard, 1993.

Paulsen, Gary. *The Cookcamp.* Orchard, 1991.

Pfeffer, Susan Beth. *Courage Dana.* Dell Paper, 1984.

Reeder, Carolyn. *Shades of Gray.* Macmillan, 1989.

Roberts, Willo Davis. *Don't Hurt Laurie!* Macmillan, 1977.

Rylant, Cynthia. *A Fine White Dust.* Macmillan, 1986.

———. *Missing May.* Orchard, 1992.

Sachar, Louis. *Dogs Don't Tell Jokes.* Alfred A. Knopf, 1991.

Sorensen, Virginia. *Plain Girl.* Scholastic, 1983.

Soto, Gary. *The Pool Party.* Delacorte Press, 1992.

Woodruff, Elvira. *The Secret Funeral of Slim Jim the Snake.* Holiday House, 1993.

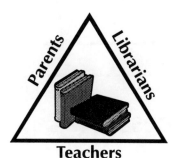

Parents
Librarians
Teachers

Chapter 11

Award Books

OVERVIEW

Thousands of children's books are published each year. With many previously published books still available, that offers an unbelievable number of titles to choose from. Of this number, only a small percentage are considered excellent. That means some of these titles are awful and many are mediocre. How does one go about locating good books for children?

It is difficult for parents to know which books are of the highest quality. A good place to start is with the award listings. For practical purposes, we limited the award books in this discussion to the more popular U.S. awards or medals.

Winning one of the honors or awards for children's books brings instant recognition to the talented author or illustrator. The excitement of the Newbery or Caldecott Award announcements, in January, spills over to the whole field of children's literature. Because award books rarely go out of print, parents can easily find these books, which is often another reason for their popularity.

GUIDED READING QUESTIONS

Choose one award and examine several of its honoree titles. Compare and contrast an older award book and a recent award book from the same list. Note your observations. Look at the format, illustrations, and vocabulary.

1. How are they different or how are they similar?

2. Why do you think the books you examined were chosen for the award they received?

3. What makes these books appealing to both boys and girls?

4. Which title appealed to you the most?

5. Which one do you think your son or daughter would like the best?

From *The Reading Connection.* © 1997. Libraries Unlimited. (800) 237-6124.

JOURNAL ARTICLE

Don't Argue with Success

There is only one way to improve the situation, and that is
to establish a program of awards for YA books similar
to the Newbery/Caldecott awards.

Several years ago at an ALA conference, I sat with Beverly Horowitz (an editor now with Bantam who has been involved in the process of publishing young adult books for a long time), who spoke of the increasing difficulty that she and other YA book editors were encountering in their attempts to produce good original hardcover YA books, particularly fiction. At the time I found this a little hard to believe; for the previous several years the annual crop of YA books had appeared to be increasing not only in quantity but in quality. However, Beverly maintained that pressures were increasing within publishing houses to increase profit margins by eliminating whatever books or kinds of books that did not turn a profit both quick and high.

Sadly enough, YA books, by their very nature, fit into this category all too well. As I pointed out in my last column, young adult hardcover books have a very limited market; the market consists, as a rule, of public libraries that have young adult collections or whose children's section stocks a certain number of books of interest to "older children." The sad figure that this translates into is an average sale of perhaps 1,500 to 2,000 books per title, except for books by a few YA superstars

By Audrey Eaglen. Reprinted with permission from *School Library Journal* (May 1990), page 54. Eaglen is Order Department Manager at the Cuyahoga County Public Library in Cleveland, OH.

such as S. E. Hinton, Richard Peck, Judy Blume, et al. These are not big numbers by any stretch of the imagination, and for that reason must be singularly unimpressive to publishers' accounting departments. Consider, also, that those 1,500 copies will most likely fail to sell for six months until the reviews appear, and you have the kind of situation that really makes bottom-liners see red. (Pun intended.)

As I said, I didn't quite believe Beverly at the time. At this past Mid-winter, however, I spoke with Stephen Roxburgh of Farrar, Straus, who not only echoed Beverly's sentiments but added that the problem of keeping YA titles in a publisher's stock as backlist is also becoming acute. He said that while the initial sale of a YA title is small, secondary sales (to add or replace copies) are almost infinitesimal, to the point where trying to convince accountants to warehouse a few hundred copies of a title on the off chance that they'll sell in a given year has become almost impossible. This then leads to another problem—if the hardcover title is not picked up by a paperback publisher (and more than half are not), then the decision to get rid of warehouse stock means that the title goes out of print, never to be seen again.

Given the size of the YA market and the other difficulties mentioned above, Roxburgh says there is only one way to improve the situation, and that is to establish a program of awards for YA books similar to the Newbery/Caldecott Awards, for several reasons. First, awards sell books; publishing people are not free with sales figures but insiders estimate that the initial sale of a Caldecott Medal winner is in excess of 50,000 copies, while the Newbery Medalist is assured of a sale of 20,000 copies or more. Honor Books are not quite so successful initially, but their sales usually far exceed sales of the average children's book.

Secondly, it is exceedingly rare for N/C award winners to go out of print. Medal winners and Honor Books usually end up as paperbacks, too—a further profit consideration. But, while it is true that the publishers of these books profit handsomely from them, the real beneficiaries are librarians, who know that they will be able to obtain additional or replacement copies for these books for their collections for the foreseeable future.

Lastly, the awards bring a great deal of attention not only to the chosen books but to the whole field of children's literature. Announcements of awards appear in metropolitan newspapers across the country, as well as on radio and TV. The books' authors are invited to discuss their work on the "Today" show and local talk shows. In short, the whole world is reminded each year that there is a whole area of literature out there called children's literature, and it is alive and well and being talked about, thank you.

The same thing could happen to YA literature, too—but only if YA people can get rid of some of the baggage of prejudice that we've been carrying around. We've long looked down our collective nose at the whole N/C awards selection process, which we've tagged with that old "elitest" label for lo these many years. Are awards "elitest" because of the insistence that quality is a valid criterion for giving awards to books? Is anyone going to give an award to a lousy book? YA people also say that the selection meetings are not democratic (that is, not open to spectators). Does this mean that YASD couldn't open its meetings process? Certainly not—Best Books has done it for years. And then, of course, the N/C banquet itself gives rise to high hilarity because of all the grande dames in white gloves and long dresses who attend it—but I probably shouldn't mention all those YA folks who don't laugh quite as hard when they themselves are invited to attend (gratis) by some publisher.

If swallowing our particular biases against the whole idea of choosing the best book or books of the year for YAs means a new lease on life for YA books through increased sales, longer in-print life and, in general, a much broader appreciation and awareness of this vital but too often overlooked genre called YA literature, then I say let's go for it. And I'm an old-line medalbasher, so that's saying something. ▲

ANNOTATED JOURNAL ARTICLES

Fiore, Carole. "Life on the Caldecott Committee," *Wilson Library Bulletin* (December 1993): 43-45.

The author describes her time on the Caldecott selection committee for 1993. She describes the process; the time spent reading and evaluating many, many books; and then the time spent to make the final decision. The author indicates some of the criteria committee members use when selecting a Caldecott winner.

Kazemek, Francis E. "What Book Awards Tell Us About Ourselves," *Education Week* (April 26, 1995): 32.

The author discusses the 1995 Caldecott winner, *Smoky Night,* written by Eve Bunting and illustrated by David Diaz. The author indicates that although this is a book for young children, the complex topic would confuse a young child. To the article's author, the book is a muddled presentation of racial issues. The illustrations are chaotic, and the stereotypical happy ending does little to make up for the book's confusing messages and lack of context.

Konigsburg, E. L. "Better Than the Nobel Prize: The Newbery Sells Books," *New York Times Book Review* (May 21, 1995): 26.

The author talks about the 1995 winner of the Newbery Medal—the only book award that guarantees a long shelf life. The author sees growth in children's book publishing since 1968, when she won the Newbery Medal. She sees children's books developing from simple to more complex forms. The importance of the Newbery Medal has been increased by more paperback books, trade books used along with basal readers in schools, and bookstores.

Sommers, Kathy. "And the Winner Is . . . Children's Choice Book Awards," *School Library Media Activities Monthly* (April 1995): 28-29, 40, 50.

The author encourages teachers and librarians to get involved in children's choice book award programs. The children serve as the judges to select the winner of the award. Many states have their own children's choice programs, which are worth looking into. Children are asked to read titles from a predetermined list. They enjoy having such an important part in the selection of a title for a book award. There are suggestions in this article for increasing students' interest in such programs.

ANNOTATED BIBLIOGRAPHY

Bunting, Eve. *Smoky Night.* Harcourt Brace Jovanovich, 1994. Caldecott Award winner 1995.

Daniel and his mother are looking out their window at people rioting in the streets below. In the middle of the night, they are awakened from sleep by cries of fire. They must evacuate their building, but Daniel is worried because he cannot find Jasmine, his cat. The neighbors and apartment dwellers are taken to a shelter for the night. At the shelter, a fireman appears with Jasmine and Mrs. Kim's big orange cat, a former enemy of Jasmine. Now the two cats drink out of the same bowl, and Daniel explains their new friendship by saying they probably didn't know each other before. The illustrations heighten the drama.

Creech, Sharon. *Walk Two Moons.* Scholastic, 1994. Newbery Award winner 1995.

This is a two-tiered story about Salamanca (Sal) Tree Hiddle and the story Sal tells of Phoebe Winterbottom. Sal travels with her grandparents from Ohio to Idaho, where Sal believes she will find her mother. Along the way, she shares the story of her friend Phoebe and how Phoebe came to know her half-brother. On the other level, Sal learns more about her mother's absence and finds out why her mother will never return from Idaho. This is a very moving book that deals with abandonment.

Cushman, Karen. *The Midwife's Apprentice*. Clarion Books, 1995. Newbery Award winner 1996.

Brat didn't have a home, a past, or a future until she met Jane the midwife. Jane Sharp discovers Brat in a warm dung heap and offers her food and a place to stay in exchange for work. Gradually Brat realizes that she has feelings and self-worth, and with perseverance she becomes the midwife's apprentice.

Fleischman, Paul. *Bull Run*. HarperCollins, 1993. Scott O'Dell Award winner 1994.

The first great battle of the Civil War is told from 16 differing points of view: through the eyes of Northerners, Southerners, generals, couriers, women, and the brave, as well as the cowardly. For instance, the book quotes Horace Greeley, the most powerful editor in the land, who sent Lincoln a letter stating that the Rebels could not be beaten after the Union lost the battle of Bull Run.

Rathmann, Peggy. *Officer Buckle and Gloria*. G. P. Putnam's Sons, 1995. Caldecott Award winner 1996.

Officer Buckle puts his school audiences to sleep during his lectures on safety. Then Gloria, the police dog, accompanies Officer Buckle and everything changes. Students pay attention and clap and cheer. Officer Buckle doesn't know that Gloria is reacting to his safety tips behind his back. What a surprise he has when he plays back a taped video of his lecture! All ends well, though, with Safety Tip 101, Always Stick with Your Buddy.

Salisbury, Graham. *Under the Blood-Red Sun*. Delacorte Press, 1994. Scott O'Dell Award winner 1995.

Tomi's grandfather and father were born in Japan but now live in Hawaii. Grandpa, impaired by a stroke, is caught between the old Japanese ways and his new life in Hawaii. Tomi loves to play baseball with his best friend Billy and the rest of the eighth-grade team. All is changed after Pearl Harbor is bombed in World War II. Mama gathers up everything to do with Japan, and they bury it in the ground. This is not enough to prevent Grandpa and Tomi's father from being imprisoned. Now it is Tomi's job to watch over his mother and younger sister.

BIBLIOGRAPHY

Jane Addams Children's Book Award

Since 1953, this award has been given annually by the Women's International League for Peace and Freedom and the Jane Addams Peace Association. This book award is given each fall to an author who has world peace and social justice as a predominant theme.

1985   Vinke, Hermann. *The Short Life of Sophie Scholl*. Harper & Row, 1984.

1986   Meltzer, Milton. *Ain't Gonna Study War No More: The Story of America's Peace Seekers*. Harper & Row, 1985.

1987   Vigna, Judith. *Nobody Wants a Nuclear War*. Whitman, 1986.

1988   Gordon, Sheila. *Waiting for the Rain*. Orchard, 1987.

1989   (Joint Winners)

Boutis, Victoria. *Looking Out*. Four Winds Press, 1988.

Hamilton, Virginia. *Anthony Burns: The Defeat and Triumph of a Fugitive Slave*. Alfred A. Knopf, 1988.

1990   McKissack, Patricia, and Frederick McKissack. *A Long Hard Journey: The Story of the Pullman Porter*. Walker, 1989.

1991   Durrell, Ann, and Marilyn Sachs. *The Big Book of Peace.* Dutton Children's Books, 1990.

1992   Buss, Fran Leeper. *Journey of the Sparrows.* Lodestar, 1991.

1993   Temple, Frances. *Taste of Salt: A Story of Modern Haiti.* Orchard, 1992.

1994   Levine, Ellen. *Freedom's Children: Young Civil Rights Activists Tell Their Own Stories.* Putnam, 1993.

1995   Freedman, Russell. *Kids at Work: Lewis Hine and the Crusade Against Child Labor.* Clarion Books, 1994.

Mildred L. Batchelder Award

This award, established in 1966, is offered by the Association for Library Service to Children, a division of the American Library Association. The award is given to an American publisher for a children's book originally published in a foreign language. It is usually awarded at the ALA midwinter meeting unless the committee feels there is no worthy recipient for that year.

1985   Orlev, Uri. *The Island on Bird Street.* Houghton Mifflin, 1984.

1986   Gallaz, Christophe, and Robert Innocenti. *Rose Blanche.* Creative Education, 1986.

1987   Frank, Rudolph. *No Hero for the Kaiser.* Lothrop, Lee & Shepard, 1986.

1988   Milsson, Ulf. *If You Didn't Have Me.* Macmillan, 1987.

1989   Hartling, Peter. *Crutches.* Lothrop, Lee & Shepard, 1988.

1990   Reuter, Bjarne. *Buster's World.* E. P. Dutton, 1989.

1991   Schami, Rafik. *A Hand Full of Stars.* Dutton Children's Books, 1987.

1992   Orlev, Uri. *The Man from the Other Side.* Houghton Mifflin, 1991.

1993   (No Award)

1994   Llorente, Pilar Molina. *The Apprentice.* Farrar, Straus & Giroux, 1993.

1995   Reuter, Bjarne. *The Boys from St. Petri.* Dutton Children's Books, 1994.

1996   Orlev, Uri. *The Lady with the Hat.* Houghton Mifflin, 1995.

Boston Globe–Horn Book Award

The *Boston Globe* newspaper and *Horn Book Magazine* established this award in 1967. Since 1976, three awards are given: one for illustrator, one for fiction or poetry, and one for nonfiction.

1985   *Fiction*
Brooks, Bruce. *The Moves Make the Man.* Harper & Row, 1987.

Nonfiction
Blumberg, Rhoda. *Commodore Perry in the Land of the Shogun.* Lothrop, Lee & Shepard, 1985.

Illustration

Hurd, Thacher. *Mama Don't Allow.* Harper & Row, 1984.

1986 *Fiction*

O'Neal, Zibby. *In Summer Light.* Viking, 1985.

Nonfiction

Thomson, Peggy. *Auks, Rocks and the Odd Dinosaur: Inside Stories from the Smithsonian's Museum of Natural History.* Thomas Y. Crowell, 1985.

Illustration

Bang, Molly. *The Paper Crane.* Greenwillow Books, 1985.

1987 *Fiction*

Lowry, Lois. *Rabble Starkey.* Houghton Mifflin, 1987.

Nonfiction

Sewall, Marcia. *Pilgrims of Plimoth.* Macmillan, 1986.

Illustration

Steptoe, John. *Mufaro's Beautiful Daughters: An African Tale.* Lothrop, Lee & Shepard, 1987.

1988 *Fiction*

Taylor, Mildred. *The Friendship.* Dial Books for Young Readers, 1987.

Nonfiction

Hamilton, Virginia. *Anthony Burns: The Defeat and Triumph of a Fugitive Slave.* Alfred A. Knopf, 1988.

Illustration

Snyder, Diane. *The Boy of the Three-Year Nap.* Houghton Mifflin, 1988.

1989 *Fiction*

Fox, Paula. *The Village by the Sea.* Franklin Watts, 1988.

Nonfiction

Macaulay, David. *The Way Things Work.* Houghton Mifflin, 1988.

Illustration

Wells, Rosemary. *Shy Charles.* Dial Books for Young Readers, 1988.

1990 *Fiction*

Spinelli, Jerry. *Maniac Magee.* Little, Brown, 1990.

Nonfiction

Fritz, Jean. *The Great Little Madison.* Putnam, 1989.

Illustration

Young, Ed. *Lon Po Po: A Red Riding Hood Story from China.* Philomel, 1989.

1991 *Fiction*

Avi. *The True Confessions of Charlotte Doyle.* Orchard, 1990.

Nonfiction

Rylant, Cynthia. *Appalachia: The Voices of Sleeping Birds.* Harcourt Brace Jovanovich, 1991.

Illustration
Paterson, Katherine. *The Tale of the Mandarin Ducks.* Lodestar, 1990.

1992 *Fiction*
Rylant, Cynthia. *Missing May.* Orchard, 1992.

Nonfiction
Cummings, Pat. *Talking with Artists.* Bradbury Press, 1992.

Illustration
Young, Ed. *Seven Blind Mice.* Philomel, 1991.

1993 *Fiction*
Berry, James. *Ajeemah and His Son.* HarperCollins, 1992.

Nonfiction
McKissack, Patricia, and Frederick McKissack. *Sojourner Truth: Ain't I a Woman?* Scholastic, 1992.

Illustration
Alexander, Lloyd. *The Fortune-Tellers.* Dutton Children's Books, 1992.

1994 *Fiction*
Williams, Vera B. *Scooter.* Greenwillow Books, 1993.

Nonfiction
Freedman, Russell. *Eleanor Roosevelt: A Life of Discovery.* Clarion Books, 1993.

Illustration
Say, Allen. *Grandfather's Journey.* Houghton Mifflin, 1993.

1995 *Fiction*
Wynne-Jones, Tim. *Some of the Kinder Planets.* Orchard, 1995.

Nonfiction
Bober, Natalie S. *Abigail Adams: Witness to a Revolution.* Atheneum, 1995.

Illustration
Lester, Julius. *John Henry.* Dial Press, 1994.

Randolph Caldecott Award

The Caldecott Award is named after a famous British illustrator, Randolph Caldecott. This annual award was the first of its kind recognizing a children's artist. This award is given for the best picture book for children published in the United States.

1985 Hodges, Margaret. *Saint George and the Dragon.* Little, Brown, 1984.

1986 Van Allsburg, Chris. *The Polar Express.* Houghton Mifflin, 1985.

1987 Yorinks, Arthur. *Hey, Al.* Farrar, Straus & Giroux, 1986.

1988 Yolen, Jane. *Owl Moon.* Philomel, 1987.

1989 Ackerman, Karen. *Song and Dance Man.* Alfred A. Knopf, 1988.

1990 Young, Ed. *Lon Po Po: A Red Riding Hood Story from China.* Philomel, 1989.

1991   Macaulay, David. *Black and White.* Houghton Mifflin, 1990.

1992   Wiesner, David. *Tuesday.* Houghton Mifflin, 1991.

1993   McCully, Emily Arnold. *Mirette on the Highwire.* Putnam, 1992.

1994   Say, Allen. *Grandfather's Journey.* Houghton Mifflin, 1993.

1995   Bunting, Eve. *Smoky Night.* Harcourt Brace Jovanovich, 1994.

1996   Rathman, Peggy. *Officer Buckle and Gloria.* G. P. Putnam's Sons, 1995.

Coretta Scott King Award

This award commemorates Dr. Martin Luther King Jr., and honors his wife Coretta Scott King for her continued work for brotherhood and world peace. The award is made to one black author and, since 1974, to one black illustrator. Their works must be educational as well as inspirational.

1985   *Author*
Myers, Walter Dean. *Motown and Didi.* Viking, 1984.

Illustrator   (No Award)

1986   *Author*
Hamilton, Virginia. *The People Could Fly: American Black Folktales.* Alfred A. Knopf, 1985.

Illustrator
Flournoy, Valerie. *The Patchwork Quilt.* Dial Books for Young Readers, 1985.

1987   *Author*
Walter, Mildred Pitts. *Justin and the Best Biscuits in the World.* Lothrop, Lee & Shepard, 1986.

Illustrator
Dragonwagon, Crescent. *Half a Moon and One Whole Star.* Macmillan, 1986.

1988   *Author*
Taylor, Mildred. *The Friendship.* Dial Books for Young Readers, 1987.

Illustrator
Steptoe, John. *Mufaro's Beautiful Daughters: An African Tale.* Lothrop, Lee & Shepard, 1987.

1989   *Author*
Myers, Walter Dean. *Fallen Angels.* Scholastic, 1988.

Illustrator
McKissack, Patricia. *Mirandy and Brother Wind.* Alfred A. Knopf, 1988.

1990   *Author*
McKissack, Patricia, and Frederick McKissack. *A Long Hard Journey: The Story of the Pullman Porter.* Walker, 1989.

Illustrator
Greenfield, Eloise. *Nathaniel Talking.* Black Butterfly Children's Books, 1988.

1991   *Author*
Taylor, Mildred D. *The Road to Memphis.* Dial Press, 1990.

Illustrator
Price, Leontyne. *Aida.* Harcourt Brace Jovanovich, 1990.

1992   *Author*
Myers, Walter Dean. *Now Is Your Time! The African American Struggle for Freedom.* HarperCollins, 1991.

Illustrator
Ringgold, Faith. *Tar Beach.* Crown, 1991.

1993   *Author*
McKissack, Patricia C. *The Dark-Thirty: Southern Tales of the Supernatural.* Alfred A. Knopf, 1992.

Illustrator
Anderson, David A. *The Origin of Life on Earth: An African Creation Myth.* Sights Productions, 1991.

1994   *Author*
Johnson, Angela. *Toning the Sweep.* Orchard, 1993.

Illustrator
Feelings, Tom. *Soul Looks Back in Wonder.* Dial Books for Young Readers, 1993.

1995   *Author*
McKissack, Patricia C., and Frederick L. McKissack. *Christmas in the Big House, Christmas in the Quarters.* Scholastic, 1994.

Illustrator
Johnson, James Weldon. *The Creation.* Holiday House, 1994.

1996   *Author*
Hamilton, Virginia. *Her Stories.* Blue Sky Press, 1995.

Illustrator
Feelings, Tom. *The Middle Passage: White Ships/Black Cargo.* Dial Books for Young Readers, 1995.

John Newbery Medal

John Newbery (1713-1766) was a British printer and bookseller, who first began publishing books for children. This award was established in 1922 and is presented to the author of the best book published for children in the preceding year.

1985   McKinley, Robin. *The Hero and the Crown.* Greenwillow Books, 1984.

1986   MacLachlan, Patricia. *Sarah, Plain and Tall.* Harper & Row, 1985.

1987   Fleischman, Sid. *The Whipping Boy.* Greenwillow Books, 1986.

1988   Freedman, Russell. *Lincoln: A Photobiography*. Clarion Books, 1987.

1989   Fleischman, Paul. *Joyful Noise: Poems for Two Voices*. Harper & Row, 1988.

1990   Lowry, Lois. *Number the Stars*. Houghton Mifflin, 1989.

1991   Spinelli, Jerry. *Maniac Magee*. Little, Brown, 1990.

1992   Naylor, Phyllis Reynolds. *Shiloh*. Atheneum, 1991.

1993   Rylant, Cynthia. *Missing May*. Orchard, 1992.

1994   Lowry, Lois. *The Giver*. Houghton Mifflin, 1993.

1995   Creech, Sharon. *Walk Two Moons*. HarperCollins, 1994.

1996   Cushman, Karen. *The Midwife's Apprentice*. Clarion Books, 1995.

Scott O'Dell Award for Historical Fiction

Author Scott O'Dell (1898-1989) originated and donated this award for a distinguished work of historical fiction. Books to be considered must be published in English by a U.S. publisher. The setting of the book must be North, Central, or South America.

1985   Avi. *The Fighting Ground*. J. B. Lippincott, 1984.

1986   MacLachlan, Patricia. *Sarah, Plain and Tall*. Harper & Row, 1985.

1987   O'Dell, Scott. *Streams to the River, River to the Sea*. Houghton Mifflin, 1986.

1988   Beatty, Patricia. *Charley Skedaddle*. William Morrow, 1987.

1989   de Jenkins, Lyll Becerra. *The Honorable Prison*. E. P. Dutton, 1988.

1990   Reeder, Carolyn. *Shades of Gray*. Macmillan, 1989.

1991   van Raven, Pieter. *A Time of Troubles*. Scribner Books for Young Readers, 1990.

1992   Hahn, Mary Downing. *Stepping on the Cracks*. Clarion Books, 1991.

1993   Dorris, Michael. *Morning Girl*. Hyperion Books for Children, 1992.

1994   Fleischman, Paul. *Bull Run*. HarperCollins, 1993.

1995   Salisbury, Graham. *Under the Blood-Red Sun*. Delacorte Press, 1994.

Laura Ingalls Wilder Award

This award was established in 1954. From 1960 to 1980, it was given every five years. Beginning in 1983, the award is made every three years to an author or illustrator whose books have made a long-lasting contribution to children's literature.

1980   Theodor S. Geisel (Dr. Seuss)

1983   Maurice Sendak

1986   Jean Fritz

1989   Elizabeth George Speare

1992   Marcia Brown

1995   Virginia Hamilton

From *The Reading Connection*. © 1997. Libraries Unlimited. (800) 237-6124.

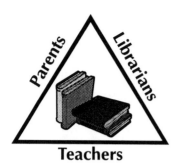
Parents
Librarians
Teachers

Chapter 12

Biographies Shape Your Future

OVERVIEW

A *biography* is the story of a person's life written by someone else. An *autobiography* is a person's story of his or her own life. Biography has long been one of the most popular forms of prose. Biographies help make the past more real and easier to understand because they tell about actual people and events. By reading biographies, people can satisfy their curiosity about well-known individuals and can experience historical events as though they were actually present.

A good biography presents the facts about a person's life. This information includes what the subject did and how the individual influenced the period in which he or she lived. A biography should also describe the subject's personality and provide an explanation for the subject's actions.

Biographers help make their writings accurate by learning as much as possible about their subjects. Biographers use such research materials as diaries, personal letters, autobiographies, and other works. A good biographical work should be objective and balanced. There are five types of biographies: popular, historical, literary, reference, and fictional.

GUIDED READING QUESTIONS

1. Is the information about the individual accurate?

2. Is the information fresh and interesting?

3. Does the author indicate what is fact and what is conjecture based on what is known about the individual?

4. Is the book a balanced presentation and an unbiased account of events and situations?

5. Is the book free of stereotypes?

6. What characteristics helped this notable person achieve his or her goals?

7. Does the book have a bibliography of sources or a list of additional readings that contributes to its credibility?

History and History Makers: Give YAs the Whole Picture

"No great man lives in vain. The history of the world is but the biography of great men." —Thomas Carlyle

History may be more than just biography, but it must include the recorded results of human considerations, choices, and actions, both at the individual and collective level. Abraham Lincoln was elected after a string of ineffective presidents, and when the Civil War broke out, he valued the Union enough to fight to preserve it. Franklin Roosevelt, considered to be a rich dilettante, overcame both the expectations of his upbringing and physical disability to change forever the American concept of government and its role in the U.S. economy. Adolf Hitler was an unsuccessful artist, so he turned his sights elsewhere, eventually starting a war that still has repercussions today.

Individuals who have influenced history are truly fascinating, but young adult readers have enormous difficulty finding out about them. We have all read and heard reports about our youths' abysmal knowledge of and interest in history, and one possible reason for this is that there are too few figures who come to life in the books they are given. As librarians, we can encourage the publication of titles that will help our students learn more about the people of the past.

By Mary E. Mueller. Reprinted with permission from *School Library Journal* (November 1991), pages 55-56. Mary Mueller is a librarian at Rolla Junior High School in Rolla, MO.

In sharp contrast to YA materials, adult titles are filled with real people whose lives are full of contradictions and fascinating character traits that influenced their actions. Who can fail to be amazed by Nixon's fall from grace, mesmerized by the charisma of John Kennedy, or awed by the brilliance of Thomas Jefferson's writings? All too often, however, the very facts that make these personalities so intriguing never make it to the YA shelves. To give credit where it is due, we have moved beyond the hero-worshipping, fictionalized, sanitized biographies that many of us were fed. They rarely made anyone, good or evil, very complex or compelling, and were often inaccurate and incomplete. As society and historical scholarship have changed, biography has changed with them. Most subjects are presented more objectively, and as a result, are more human and interesting. However, the books often include too much detail about the person's early life and tend to overlook or omit controversial information.

In spite of their flaws, most biographies fare quite well when compared with books about history. Far too many of them are little more than expanded compilations of events, with no discussion or detail about those who shaped them. When the personalities are taken out of history, there is little left to help teens understand why things have happened as they have. As examples, very few titles about the '60s, the civil rights movement, or the Vietnam War examine in any detail the rich, complex character of Lyndon Johnson, a man who greatly influenced all three and who is extremely important to any understanding of these happenings and the era in which they occurred.

We all know that YA nonfiction cannot be expected to cover as much ground as its adult counterpart. Teens rarely have the reading skills, background knowledge, or interest to enjoy or benefit greatly from it. But they do deserve books that examine both the participants and events of the past and tie them together in a way that allows readers to see a cause and effect relationship. As librarians, we can do several things to help students obtain and use solid, involving, and accurate information.

First, we need to pay more attention to the 900s sections in our libraries. It is far too easy to tell ourselves that since a person lived 200 years ago, a 25-year-old book is still acceptable. After all, in an era of tight budgets, it is easier to justify new titles in the computer section. But there has been such a change in perspective in those areas in the last few years that books published in the '60s (and earlier) are as outdated as the science and computer books of that time. Attitudes and outlooks have undergone massive change, to say nothing of revisionists' theories. We can weed so ruthlessly that what we have on our shelves is current and readable.

Second, we can make our opinions heard. We can encourage publishers, jobbers, and sales staffs to give us books that offer a fuller, more insightful perspective. And since nothing speaks as loudly as our acquisitions dollars, we must buy only the good titles and reject the rest. We can read and use reviews to have a wish list on hand so when the parents or friends' groups want to help, we can update these important sections immediately.

Third, we can take a realistic attitude toward prominent figures. Many of us are afraid to put controversial materials on our shelves. But our past and present are full of personages who lived outside traditional rules. They often used poor judgment or acted in a less-than-exemplary fashion. Failure to include that type of information makes books boring or inaccurate. Many authors whitewash and even change language that contains profanity, which takes away a sense of how a biographical subject thought and spoke. How can we expect our students to really see the personality of Harry Truman without letting them see the tenacity, salty language, and temper that so characterized him? We can buy books that treat individuals and occurrences with honesty and insight, even when they contain profanity, examine bad behavior or dirty tricks, or pose a picture of established heroes as having feet of clay.

Fourth, and most importantly, we can act as facilitators. When students need information about the American Revolution, we should recommend a biography as well as a book from 973.3. This does require some work and extra reading on our part, but it will pay off very quickly in better student understanding and library use. Many of us routinely read the new fiction so that we can be aware of any "surprises" found within or so that we can recommend or booktalk it. We can also take the time to read history and biography. Students will be amazed when librarians offer anecdotes or tidbits about the person they are researching, or tell them a little known fact about an event or historical era.

Dubowski's *Robert E. Lee and the Rise of the South,* Rickarby's *Ulysses S. Grant and the Strategy of Victory,* and Shorto's *Abraham Lincoln* (all Silver Burdett, 1991) do a fine job of combining these two topics. They describe in detail how a single individual changed the course of history and made a difference. Other titles in this "The History of the Civil War" series offer more diversity, highlighting such figures as *Clara Barton* by Dubowski, *Harriet Tubman* by McClard, and *John C. Calhoun and the Roots of War* by Celsi.

For those needing material about the early years of America, an excellent introductory title is Marrin's *Struggle for a Continent: The French and Indian Wars* (1987), which is followed by his *The War for Independence* (1988, both Atheneum). The two can be combined with Milton Meltzer's *George Washington and the Birth of Our Nation* (1986), *Benjamin Franklin: The New American* (1988), and *Thomas Jefferson: The Revolutionary Aristocrat* (1991, all Watts) for a very full examination of those who played key roles in shaping the new nation. The last title, in particular, contains an intelligent discussion of the problems slavery posed for Jefferson personally as well as the new country. Doris and Harold Faber's *The Birth of a Nation* (Scribner's, 1989) and Marrin's *1812: The War Nobody Won* (Atheneum, 1985) move readers beyond the earliest years of the republic.

Scott's *John Brown of Harper's Ferry* (Facts on File, 1988), an excellent treatment, looks at the passions surrounding the slavery issue, and shows readers how the obsessions of a single man helped bring on the Civil War.

All libraries serving adolescents have World War II buffs. Marrin's brilliant *Hitler* (1987) and *Stalin* (1988, both Viking) can add greatly to an understanding of how evil the two men actually were and his look at their monstrous behavior is both fascinating and repelling.

For students of African-American history, there are many figures who labored hard for civil rights gains whose lives have been chronicled. Aldred's *Thurgood Marshall* (Chelsea House, 1990) details his subject's ceaseless efforts on the behalf of those who needed help, and Bernard's *Journey Toward Freedom: The Story of Sojourner Truth* (Feminist Pr., 1990) provides a different perspective on the struggles black women had not only with the white world, but also with black men.

A real perspective on how Vietnam divided our country can be found in Warren's *Portrait of a Tragedy* (Lothrop, 1990) and the Hooblers' *Vietnam: Why We Fought* (Knopf, 1990). Both books view the entire war as a disaster, but differ greatly in their treatment of North Vietnamese and U.S. motivations and placement of blame for the entire debacle. Although many books are available on Kennedy—Judie Mill's *John F. Kennedy* (Watts, 1988) is among the best—many of us are still waiting for a good YA treatment of Johnson that explains why he conducted the war as he did.

Almost all libraries contain at least some books that can help students appreciate any aspect or era of history more. Take some time and become more familiar with what your library has to offer and provide your students with titles that are more than just listings of trivia. Put those fascinating people back into history. ▲

ANNOTATED JOURNAL ARTICLES

Freedman, Russell. "Bring 'Em Back Alive," *School Library Journal* (March 1994): 138-41.

The author thinks of himself as a storyteller and does his best to bring dramatic shape to his subject in a clear, simple, and forceful manner. A biography should develop the character by creating convincing word pictures. The use of quotations can give a story a sense of reality. Another essential storytelling device is the use of anecdotes.

Girard, Linda Walvoord. "Biography and Lore," *Horn Book Magazine* (November/December 1990): 708-13.

Biographies began by building emotional reference points, not just by relaying information and facts. Oral history—"lore"—is relied upon to help sketch the subjects. Lore helps to make a biography more memorable and brings reality and immediacy to biographies because every life includes some unlikely events or moments.

Moore, Ann W. "Beyond the Surface: Problems and Challenges in Young Adult Biographies," *School Library Journal* (August 1990): 94-95.

A good biography is more than a recital of events. It is stimulating, with a central theme and a close examination of the subject personality. The author relates four common problems with biographies: an overabundance of unimportant details, a failure to flesh out facts, an absence of basics, and bending over backward to avoid bias.

ANNOTATED BIBLIOGRAPHY

Anderson, William. *A Biography of Laura Ingalls Wilder.* HarperCollins, 1992.

This biography details Laura's adult life with her husband, Almanzo, and their daughter, Rose. When she was more than 60 years old, she began to write about her pioneer adventures. "I had seen the whole frontier," Laura wrote, "the woods, the Indian country of the great plains, the frontier towns, the building of railroads in wild, unsettled country, homesteading and farms coming in to take possession. I realized that I had seen and lived it all—all the successive phases of the frontier, first the frontiersman, then the pioneer, then the farmers, and the towns."

Demi. *Chingis Khan.* Henry Holt, 1991.

Chingis, which means "spirit of light," unified all the Mongols and conquered China, Persia, and Russia. He established the greatest continuous land empire in history. The Persians said, "He is over eighteen feet tall, more powerful than three bulls, and one of his arrows can pierce twenty men." Chingis died in 1227, at the age of 67, from a hunting wound inflicted by a wild boar.

Kroll, Steven. *By the Dawn's Early Light: The Story of the Star-Spangled Banner.* Scholastic, 1994.

During the War of 1812, Francis Scott Key was a prominent lawyer in Washington. The British had just burned down a defenseless Washington and taken prisoner Dr. William Beanes, who was a dear friend of Key. Francis received permission to visit the British fleet to plead for his friend's release. Instead, he was forced to remain aboard the British ship as it attacked Fort McHenry. Who would have possession of the fort in the morning? It was in the dawn's early light, when the Stars and Stripes could be seen, that an inspired Francis Scott Key wrote "The Star-Spangled Banner."

Lasky, Kathryn. *The Librarian Who Measured the Earth.* Little, Brown, 1994.

When Eratosthenes measured the circumference of the earth more than 2,000 years ago, his calculation was only 200 miles off. He was a man full of curiosity and head librarian of the library at Alexandria. Much of what is known about Eratosthenes is pieced together, because he left behind no personal accounts or journals, despite all the volumes he wrote.

Lyons, Mary E. *Stitching Stars: The Story Quilts of Harriet Powers.* Charles Scribner's Sons, 1993.

Harriet Powers was born and raised as a plantation slave. She married when she was 18 and had 11 children. Over the years she sewed many quilts. Around 1886 she began her Bible quilt, now a treasure in the Smithsonian Institute. It is made up of 299 appliquéd pieces of cloth. Scenes from Harriet Powers's quilts are found on almost every page of this informative book.

Stevens, Bryna. *Frank Thomson: Her Civil War Story.* Macmillan, 1992.

Emma Edmonds disguised herself as a man and joined the Union side of the Civil War. Known as Frank Thomson, she served as a nurse and then a mail carrier. She volunteered to be a spy and donned several disguises, including that of a female slave. Eventually she deserted the Union Army, and no one knows why. Perhaps after defying tradition for many years, she just wanted to be a woman again.

BIBLIOGRAPHY

Adler, David A. *A Picture Book of Harriet Tubman.* Holiday House, 1992.

Applegate, Katherine. *The Story of Two American Generals.* Dell Paper, 1992.

Ashabranner, Brent. *People Who Make a Difference.* E. P. Dutton, 1989.

Blos, Joan W. *The Days Before Now: An Autobiographical Note by Margaret Wise Brown.* Simon & Schuster, 1994.

Bober, Natalie S. *Abigail Adams.* Atheneum Books for Young Readers, 1995.

Brooks, Polly S. *Queen Eleanor, Independent Spirit of the Medieval World: A Biography of Eleanor of Aquitaine.* J. B. Lippincott, 1983.

Bulla, Clyde Robert. *Pocahontas and the Strangers.* Scholastic, 1971.

Burleigh, Robert. *Flight: The Journey of Charles Lindbergh.* Philomel, 1991.

Coerr, Eleanor. *Sadako and the Thousand Paper Cranes.* Putnam, 1977.

Cummings, Pat. *Talking with Artists.* Bradbury Press, 1992.

Dahl, Roald. *Boy: Tales of Childhood.* Farrar, Straus & Giroux, 1984.

Demi. *Chingis Khan.* Henry Holt, 1991.

Downing, Julie. *Mozart Tonight.* Bradbury Press, 1991.

Everston, Jonathan. *Colin Powell.* Bantam Paper, 1991.

Faber, Doris, and Harold Faber. *Nature and the Environment; Great Lives.* Macmillan, 1991.

Fisher, Leonard Everett. *Marie Curie.* Macmillan, 1994.

——. *Prince Henry the Navigator.* Macmillan, 1990.

Freedman, Russell. *Eleanor Roosevelt: A Life of Discovery.* Clarion Books, 1993.

——. *Indian Chiefs.* Holiday House, 1987.

——. *Lincoln: A Photobiography.* Clarion Books, 1987.

——. *The Wright Brothers: How They Invented the Airplane.* Holiday House, 1991.

Fritz, Jean. *The Double Life of Pocahontas.* Putnam, 1983.

——. *Homesick: My Own Story.* Putnam, 1982.

——. *Make Way for Sam Houston.* Putnam, 1986.

——. *What's the Big Idea, Ben Franklin?* Coward-McCann, 1976.

Gallardo, Evelyn. *Among the Orangutans: The Birute Galdikas Story.* Chronicle Books, 1993.

Giblin, James Cross. *George Washington: A Picture Book Biography.* Scholastic, 1992.

Giff, Patricia Reilly. *Laura Ingalls Wilder, Growing Up in the Little House.* Viking Kestrel, 1987.

Harrison, Barbara, and Daniel Terris. *A Twilight Struggle: The Life of John Fitzgerald Kennedy.* Lothrop, Lee & Shepard, 1992.

Hautzig, Esther. *The Endless Steppe: Growing Up in Siberia.* HarperCollins, 1968.

Huynh, Quang Nhuong. *The Land I Lost: Adventures of a Boy in Vietnam.* HarperCollins, 1982.

Jerome, Leah. *Dian Fossey.* Bantam Paper, 1991.

Keegan, Marcia. *Pueblo Boy: Growing Up in Two Worlds.* Cobblehill, 1991.

Krull, Kathleen. *Lives of the Writers: Comedies, Tragedies (And What the Neighbors Thought).* Harcourt Brace Jovanovich, 1994.

Kunhardt, Edith. *Honest Abe.* Greenwillow Books, 1993.

Latham, Jean Lee. *Carry On, Mr. Bowditch.* Houghton Mifflin, 1955.

Leitner, Isabella. *The Big Lie: A True Story.* Scholastic, 1992.

Lipsyte, Robert. *Joe Louis: A Champ for All America.* HarperCollins, 1994.

McKissack, Patricia. *Jessie Jackson.* Scholastic, 1989.

———. *Sojourner Truth: Ain't I a Woman?* Scholastic, 1992.

McLanathan, Richard B. *Leonardo da Vinci.* Harry N. Abrams, 1990.

Meyer, Susan E. *Edgar Degas.* Harry N. Abrams, 1994.

Monjo, F. N. *The One Bad Thing About Father.* Harper Paper, 1970.

Moore, Eva. *The Story of George Washington Carver.* Scholastic, 1971.

Morris, Ann. *Dancing to America.* Dutton Children's Books, 1994.

O'Neal, Zibby. *Grandma Moses: Painter of Rural America.* Viking Kestrel, 1986.

Peet, Bill. *Bill Peet: An Autobiography.* Houghton Mifflin, 1989.

Pinkney, Andrea Davis. *Alvin Ailey.* Hyperion Books for Children, 1993.

Pringle, Laurence. *Batman: Exploring the World of Bats.* Charles Scribner's Sons, 1991.

Provensen, Alice. *The Buck Stops Here: The Presidents of the United States.* HarperCollins, 1990.

Provensen, Alice, and Martin Provensen. *The Glorious Flight: Across the Channel with Louis Bleriot.* Viking Press, 1983.

Rappaport, Doreen. *Living Dangerously: American Women Who Risked Their Lives for Adventure.* HarperCollins, 1991.

Raschka, Chris. *Charlie Parker Played BeBop.* Orchard, 1992.

Retan, Walter. *Daniel Boone: Wilderness Explorer.* Dell, 1992.

Say, Allen. *El Chino.* Houghton Mifflin, 1990.

Sills, Leslie. *Inspirations: Stories About Women Artists.* Whitman, 1989.

Simon, Charnan. *Janet Reno: First Woman Attorney General.* Childrens Press, 1994.

Sis, Peter. *Follow the Dream.* Alfred A. Knopf, 1991.

St. George, Judith. *Dear Dr. Bell . . . Your Friend, Helen Keller.* Putnam, 1992.

Stanley, Diane, and Peter Vennema. *Bard of Avon: The Story of William Shakespeare.* Morrow Junior Books, 1992.

———. *Cleopatra.* Morrow Junior Books, 1992.

Stanley, Fay. *The Last Princess: The Story of Princess Ka'iulani of Hawai'i.* Four Winds Press, 1991.

Sullivan, George. *Sluggers.* Macmillan, 1991.

Turner, Robyn. *Georgia O'Keeffe.* Little, Brown, 1991.

Van der Rol, Ruud, and Rian Verhoeven. *Anne Frank, Beyond the Diary: A Photographic Remembrance.* Viking, 1993.

White, Nancy Bean. *Meet John F. Kennedy.* Random House, 1965.

Wisniewski, David. *Sundiata: Lion King of Mali.* Clarion Books, 1992.

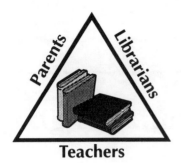

Chapter 13

Series for Everyone

OVERVIEW

Researchers have found that young readers like stereotyped characters and are comforted by sameness and simplicity in characters and plots. The series book does not demand analysis, and the content does not challenge a child's reading ability. The stories move along quickly, many with a bit of suspense or intrigue at the end of each of the short chapters to keep readers interested. The stories have lots of dialogue and keep narrative description to a minimum.

Books in a series usually have the same covers, the same main characters, and the same reading level, and are usually about the same length. Readers like the idea of a character being in control or being able to retaliate—with limitations. The setting is usually one where any number of different characters and situations can fit easily.

Many adults consider series books to be new and dangerous developments, but actually they have been around for a long time. Series, stories about the same characters, come in a wide variety of topics, from the Bobbsey Twins to Nancy Drew. There's something for everyone!

GUIDED READING QUESTIONS

Pick one series and examine a few of the titles.

1. What makes the series you chose popular?

2. Are the main characters well rounded and "real," or can they be defined in terms of one characteristic (such as good, bad, popular, etc.)?

3. What is the setting?

4. Are the stories predictable?

5. Are important social issues brought up (such as prejudice, divorce, or other social concerns)?

6. Is the ending satisfying?

JOURNAL ARTICLE

Why Girls Flock to Sweet Valley High

After several months of research on teenage
romance fiction, I no longer view *Sweet Valley High*
as a threat. I will not be overly concerned
if my daughter lingers there a while longer.

What do you do when your good reader, that eager consumer of a couple of stacks of library books per week, suddenly changes her habits? The hardcovers with their appealing jackets sit untouched, even the ones marked YA with the more grown-up subject matter. Instead, the drawerful of skimpy-looking paperbacks with the rosy-cheeked blonds on the covers get all the attention. As a librarian-in-the-making, I recognized the signs of the preadolescent paperback fetish, but as a parent I couldn't face the fact that my 11-year-old daughter had fallen prey to formula romances. Fortunately for me, there were papers to be written, research to be done. Why not, I thought, attack the problem head on—find out why these books attract and hold their audience and what, if anything, can be done to broaden the reading habits of formula fans?

The first point my research uncovered was that my daughter and her friends were not alone in their enthusiasm for *Sweet Valley High* and other romances. In every survey I found, girls consistently listed romances when asked to name the kinds of books they preferred.[1] Berta Parrish of Arizona State surveyed 250 eighth- through twelfth-grade students from three schools. She found that 70 percent of eleventh-grade girls had read five or more romances during the previous year. In the twelfth grade, 55 percent had read at least five romances, but 12 percent had read 30 or more romances that year.[2] In a survey of 844 students in ten New York City high schools, 73 percent of female students preferred romance books.[3] Among rural North Carolina students surveyed by Constance Mellon, 90 percent of the girls listed romance as their favorite reading category.[4]

Girls not only show a preference for these books when surveyed, they vote for them in the marketplace with their own dollars. A *Publishers Weekly* telephone survey of a representative sample of 13- to 18-year-olds found that 44 percent of the girls interviewed purchased romance books during one week in 1986.[5] When *Publishers Weekly* talked two years earlier with managers of bookstores with large young adult sections, they reported a similarly high volume of sales. One bookseller said that he had sold 200 to 300 *Sweet Valley Highs* per week during a promotional contest sponsored by the books' publisher, Bantam.[6]

By Mary M. Huntwork. Reprinted by permission from *School Library Journal* (March 1990), pages 137-40. Mary M. Huntwork is a graduate student in the Department of Instructional Technology and Library Science at Marshall University, Huntington, WV.

In 1986, the first young adult novel ever to reach the *New York Times* paperback best-seller list was a *Sweet Valley High* Super Edition (slightly heftier variation) called *Perfect Summer.* Four years later the books continue to make the charts. The September 29, 1989 *Publishers Weekly* children's bestseller list showed *Broken-hearted (Sweet Valley High #58)* in third place in the young adult division. By the end of 1989 there were 34 million *Sweet Valley High* books in print in the United States. The books appear in 15 languages.

Obviously, superior marketing answers a large part of my question about why girls read these books. Bantam has followed the historically successful formula in the paperback industry—predictability equals profit. If publishers can identify a category of book and the people who seek that category, then they can predict sales and avoid costly mistakes. Following the adult romance tradition, Bantam targeted an audience, determined what that audience wanted, and made it readily and widely available.

The staying power of books written by Beverly Cleary and Betty Cavanna and several others in the 1950s and before, showed that there was a market for teenage romance books waiting to be tapped. Bantam joined the romance revival in the early 1980s with the *Sweet Dreams* series. Bantam's Judy Gitenstein told *Publishers Weekly* in July 1985 that "By the time *Sweet Valley High* was ready [in 1983], the marketing department was more than ready to deal with it aggressively. As each book came out, it claimed the number one spot on [B. Dalton's] 'Hooked on Books' YA list." Marketing efforts included teen magazine promotions, newspaper advertising, contests, and giveaways.

When teenage girls got word of the new books, they did not have to go farther than the book rack at their nearest super-market, drugstore, discount chain, or mall to find them. And no matter how large or crowded the rack, *Sweet Valley High* books stand out immediately. The pastel covers (at least a dozen different shades), the circle crowned with the series title and encompassing the portrait of the main characters, and the provocative titles all reach the browser from six feet away. Closer up, potential readers get an idea of the plot from the details of the portrait and from the questions beneath: Has Jessica found someone new? Will Elizabeth lose her best friend? Some teen romance publishers use photographs on the covers, but designers at Scholastic and Bantam now consider color portraits with photographic realism more romantic looking.

Features such as the small pennant on the cover bearing the number of the book, the lists and order forms for other titles, and the hook paragraphs at the end of each novel leading into the next story, all emphasize the serial nature of the books. The series approach appeals to the "collect all twelve" mentality most children have grown up with. A phrase Roger Sutton once used in an *SLJ* piece [May 1984] put a new focus on the books for me. Sutton said that reading one of the choose-your-own-ending romances is more "like playing with a Barbie Doll than hoping and suffering along with the heroine." Barbie and *Sweet Valley High's* Wakefield twins belong to the same fantasy consumer world. Just about the time girls outgrow Barbie at age 10 or 11, the Wakefields step in to take their place.

What I learned about teenage romances as consumer items confirmed my preconceptions of the books as skillfully marketed junk food. I had no trouble finding sources critical of their literary merit or redeeming social value—particularly during the early 1980s, when the series romances began to flourish. Critics of the books commonly named these characteristics: poor character development; weak writing; use of stereotypes; emphasis on superficial and materialistic values (clothes, make-up, cars, popularity, physical appearance); sexism (female characters find value only in relation to boyfriends); and finally, failure to reflect real life (predominance of white, middle-class characters, facile solutions to dilemmas).

Journalist Margo Jefferson wrote one of the most scathing commentaries. She faulted the books for promoting the "notion that a threatening world can be made benign and orderly through external means (magic and fate) or internal means (conformity and submission). . . . What these books are really marketing is wishful thinking—the state of mind many teenagers are in when they experience intercourse, pregnancy, abortion, or childbirth."[7]

Armed with criticisms like these, I felt a bit smug in my approach to the books. However, as I consulted *Genreflecting: A Guide to Reading Interests in Genre Fiction* (Libraries Unlimited, 1986), a reference book on adult romances, I was brought up short by the following dedication page quote: Rosenberg's First Law of Reading—*Never apologize for your reading tastes.* Thus, Betty Rosenberg, author of the guide and senior lecturer emerita, UCLA Graduate School of Library Science, set the tone for the next phase of my research.

This nonjudgmental attitude also predominated in an eye- and mind-opening book by Janice Radway, *Reading the Romance: Women, Patriarchy, and Popular Literature* (University of North Carolina Press, 1984). Radway asserts that critics cannot explain why women read romances just by examining the books themselves. She rejects the idea that the text of a book is a fixed object. The reader, she says, brings assumptions and strategies to the book that give the text meaning.

In order to learn what the readers brought to the novels and what they gained from their reading experiences, Radway studied 42 women who read a specific type of romance. On one level, the romances seemed to provide "a utopian vision in which female individuality and a sense of self are shown to be compatible with nurturance and care by another." Vicariously, through the novels, the women see their mates transformed by love from dominant and insensitive to nurturing and caring individuals.

In addition, Radway theorized that a romance functions both as a novel and as mythology. Reading a romance, like oral myth telling, is a "ritual of hope" in which the same events occur again and again in the same pattern. Yet the romances also function as novels with characters and situations that seem new with each story. Even though teen romances differ greatly from their adult counterparts, Radway's reader response approach and her view of romance as mythology offer new ways to look at these young adult formula books.

Mary Anne Moffitt, of the University of Illinois, took a similar approach in her study of 14 high school girls from a white-collar, middle-class community.[8] She used open-ended questionnaires followed by 45-minute interviews of avid romance readers. Five of the girls were interviewed a second time. The girls read a minimum of two books a month, with most reading six to 20 romances in that time. Most of them read *Harlequins* and other adult romances, but one-third also read *Sweet Valley High* and other teen romances.

Moffitt observed that the girls surveyed felt strong identification with main characters. Some stated that they briefly "became" or pretended to be that character. The romance provided "a portable and intensely absorbing fantasy escape," Moffitt wrote. "The struggle they feel between what family and society expect of them and what they feel capable of accomplishing is managed in one way, through this leisure reading practice."

Interest in the opposite sex motivates romance reading. The girls indicated that they liked the long conversations between the male and female characters and descriptions of what boys were thinking. They also liked fights in which the girl spoke her mind without ending a relationship. Moffitt wrote that the books helped the girls capture a feeling of being in love and being loved. In a way, the girls could try out life (personal relationships, developing a sense of self, breaking with parents) through their reading.

Moffitt made some interesting comments on fantasy and reality. Children accept fantasy-as-truth in their reading, she said, while adolescents read the novels as *understood fantasy*. Perhaps this process accounts for adolescent acceptance of plots and solutions that seem unrealistic to adults. Also, Moffitt's subjects explained how they exerted control over the text, constructing their own images if they were not pleased with story details (such as hair color, for example).

Both Moffitt and Radway emphasized the satisfaction and pleasure romance readers receive from leisure reading. Another study, however, pointed up society's mixed feelings about this pleasure. Victor Nell conducted several studies over six years on the psychology of reading for pleasure. Nell concluded:

> It is a strange reflection of our culture that pleasure reading, so zealously inculcated by school reading programs, may later be judged by the products of this education as aesthetically worthless, in society's eyes, if not in their own.[9]

In one study, Nell asked 33 pleasure readers to indicate what percentage of their reading might be rated as trash by someone like their high school English teacher. The mean ranking was 42.6 percent. Twelve of the readers rated 75 percent of their reading as trash.[10]

Constance Mellon found a similar situation in her *SLJ* study. Eighteen percent of the rural students she surveyed answered "no" when asked if they read in their spare time. Elsewhere in the questionnaire, though, almost half of these students said that they read newspapers, sports, mysteries, romances and the like. "The respondents frequently seemed to consider things that interested them not quite legitimate categories," Mellon noted.

Nell also found wide agreement among people with language, gender and career differences about what constitutes good pleasure reading. However, when the same group of people rated book excerpts for merit, the difficult passages, not the most enjoyable ones, ranked highest. Preference and merit were inversely related. Nell sees the Protestant ethic at work here, with pain and virtue as constant companions and the best medicine tasting worst. Does the idea that pleasure reading is a waste of time and money lurk over certain pronouncements about *Sweet Valley High*?

Many reading specialists who choose to write about romance reading do not condemn it as a worthless activity. Instead, they seem to share a practical attitude. Formula fiction, they might say, will always be with us. Why not use the books to motivate readers and fight aliteracy? As reading educator Lucy Fuchs put it, "Out of these early reading experiences will come the habit of reading.... By accepting their reading choices at this sensitive age and by talking to them about what they have read, we can provide them with perspectives on love and life."[11]

Not all librarians in the trenches are threatened by *Sweet Valley High* books, either. In a Jan./Feb. 1988 *Book Report* article titled "You Can't Make Them Read Anything," Sherry York urged librarians to "Respect the individual student and his or her needs. Never mind that you'd like to see Janie read at least one hardcover sometime this year. If Janie is reading paperback romances ad nauseum, at least she has recognized that reading is a pleasurable activity, and she might even expand her vocabulary."

After several months of research on teenage romance fiction, I too no longer view *Sweet Valley High* as a threat. I will not be overly concerned if my daughter lingers there a while longer. Still, doubts remain. I found no study that assessed the reading habits of teen romance readers two, five, or ten years after they have outgrown the books. What accounts for the difference between those young people who move on to *Harlequins* and those who branch out into many kinds of pleasure reading?

I suspect that reading mentors—teachers, librarians, parents, and friends—make a difference. In Andrea Sledge's description of the ideal mentor, I found a model for the librarian/romance-reader relationship. Sledge describes reading mentors as "close, trusted, experienced counselors and guides in the development and promotion of a wide variety of reading interests." [12]

Part of building trust, of course, is acceptance, not only of the adolescents themselves, but of their reading choices. Each time a girl selects a *Sweet Valley High* book, she is telling us something. Publishers know this and have listened closely. The strong response to their romance series told them that not all teenagers identify with the characters of the heavier problem novels, that some teenagers want to read about situations closer to their own. Publishers responded not only with more series books, but with changes in their young adult trade books as well. Likewise *Sweet Valley High* readers told publishers that they liked buying books in

convenient places. Now we are beginning to see more quality children's and young adult paperbacks in the discount stores.

Taking a cue from the publishers, reading mentors also need to listen carefully to the echoes from *Sweet Valley High*.

Notes

1. Gallo, Donald R. "Reading Interests and Habits of Connecticut Students in Grades 4-12." (ERIC Document Reproduction Service No. ED 244 233, March 1984). Ross, Beth, and Nancy Simone. "Reading Interests of Tenth, Eleventh, and Twelfth Grade Students." (ERIC Document Reproduction Service No. 215 329, April 1982). Thomason, Nevada. "Survey Reveals Truth About Young Adult Readers." (ERIC Document Reproduction Service No. ED 237 959, 1983).

2. Parrish, Berta. "Enticing Readers: The Teen Romance Craze." Presentation to the International Reading Association Annual Meeting, Atlanta, May 1984. (ERIC Document Reproduction Service No. ED 245 1986).

3. Bank, Stanley. "Assessing Reading Interests of Adolescent Students." *Educational Research Quarterly* 10:3 (1986), pp. 8-13.

4. Mellon, Constance A. "Teenagers Do Read: What Youth Say About Leisure Reading." *School Library Journal* 33 (February 1987), pp. 27-30.

5. Wood, Leonard A. "How Teenage Book Tastes Change." *Publishers Weekly* 230 (22 August 1986), p. 39.

6. Roback, Diane. "Selling Young Adult Books." *Publishers Weekly* 226 (19 October 1984), pp. 24-27.

7. Jefferson, Margo. "Sweet Dreams for Teen Queens." *The Nation* 234 (22 May 1982), pp. 613-17.

8. Moffitt, Mary Anne. "Understanding the Appeal of the Romance Novel for the Adolescent Girl: A Reader-Response Approach." Presentation to the International Communications

Association Conference, Montreal, May 1987. (ERIC Document Reproduction Service No. ED 284 190).

9. Nell, Victor. "The Psychology of Reading for Pleasure." *Reading Research Quarterly* 23 (Winter 1988), pp. 21.

10. Nell, Victor. *Lost in a Book: The Psychology of Reading for Pleasure.* Yale University Press, 1988, pp. 4-5.

11. Fuchs, Lucy. "Serving Adolescents' Reading Interests through Young Adult Litera-ture." Presentation to the Phi Delta Kappa Educational Foundation, Bloomington, IN, 1987. (ERIC Document Reproduction Service No. ED 289 159).

12. Sledge, Andrea Celine. "This Book Reminds Me of You: The Reader as Mentor (Maintaining and Expanding the Range of Reading Interests)." Presentation to the International Reading Association Annual Meeting, Atlanta, May 1984. (ERIC Document Reproduction Service No. 259 303). ▲

ANNOTATED JOURNAL ARTICLES

Cooper, Ilene. "Sweet Are the Uses of Predictability," *New York Times Book Review* (November 8, 1992): 52.

The author reminds us that series books have a long, successful history; remember the adventures of some of the old-time favorites? The article has summaries of some series and a few thoughts about what makes each series popular.

Fong, Doris. "From Sweet Valley They Say We Are Leaving . . ." *School Library Journal* (January 1990): 38-39.

Don't try to defend the literary merit of teen romances. Formula romances give young readers a sense of empowerment as they struggle to both resist and challenge the pressures of society. Instead, look for books with well-rounded characters who have a sense of humor. A perfect boy needs some flaws, for true-to-life teen experiences, and girls should be concerned about SATs, grades, sports, and career plans.

Makowski, Silk. "Serious About Series: Selection Criteria for a Neglected Genre," *VOYA* (February 1994): 349-51.

The author states that series are a genre unto themselves; therefore, they should be treated as such and not compared to monographs. She also notes that all aspects of a successful series provide longevity and continuity. All series are predictable. As adults, we only need to read one to get an idea of the series.

Pennebaker, Ruth. "Why Girls Can't Get Enough of The Baby-Sitter's Club," *Parents Magazine* (June 1994): 93-94.

The Baby-Sitter's Club is a popular series because it explores subjects that kids commonly fantasize about, such as romance, sudden danger, and mystery. This all exists in a cozy, predictable world with simple answers. Series books allow kids to experience things, such as divorce, eating disorders, the death of a loved one, life as a teenager, making money, and going on dates, at a safe distance. Many people are comforted by the fact that any reading improves vocabulary, spelling, and creativity or imagination.

ANNOTATED BIBLIOGRAPHY

Dixon, Franklin. *The Serpent's Tooth Mystery.* Pocket Books, 1988. (The Hardy Boys #93)

Venomous snakes have escaped from the zoo, and Dr. Michaels has been critically injured by a poison dart. Joe and Frank Hardy try to solve the case and help their friend Phil, who is the chief suspect. The case hinges on finding the man who consistently folds scrap paper, tickets, and the like in a particular way.

Hope, Laura Lee. *The Case of the Crooked Contest.* Pocket Books, 1989. (The New Bobbsey Twins #11)

Flossie and Freddie, the younger Bobbsey twins, and their older brother, Bert, are videotaping the Greenwood gymnastic cup finals. Nan, Bert's twin, is helping out on the floor. The local favorite is Mary Lee Chin. Strange things are happening, and the evidence all points to Mary Lee Chin. It is up to the Bobbsey twins to find who is stealing and cheating in order to win the Greenwood cup.

Hughes, Dean. *Superstar Team.* Alfred A. Knopf, 1991. (Angel Park All-Stars #9)

This year the Dodgers are going to take the district tournament—or are they? The Dodgers could talk a good game, but could they win the games? It is the talk that worries Kenny. They are overconfident. It worries the coach also, which is why he benches the three best players. Will it work? Will they finally pull together as a team, or are their individual statistics more important? Pictures and statistics of the team members are included at the end of the book. There is also a short biography of one of the players, the All-Star of the Month.

John, Laurie. *He's Watching You.* Bantam Books, 1995. (Sweet Valley University: Thriller Edition)

The Sweet Valley twins are freshmen at Sweet Valley University. They are involved in a mystery right from the beginning. Jessica is recovering from an attempted rape by a star football player, while Elizabeth is reeling from an attempted murder by William White, a psychopath. What Elizabeth doesn't know is that William has not given up his romantic fantasy. He stalks Elizabeth, leaving gruesome clues, murder, and terror in his wake.

Martin, Ann M. *Karen's School Picture.* Scholastic, 1989. (Baby-Sitters Little Sister #5)

Karen Two-Two has two of everything. She has two houses and families (one at each house). Most of the time, she stays with her mother at the little house. Every other weekend, she goes to visit her father at the big house. Karen likes going to the big house. There is always something going on. Lately Karen has noticed that she gets a headache every time she tries to read. Karen needs glasses; in fact, she needs two pairs. She wears one for reading and one for seeing at a distance. Karen doesn't mind the glasses, but how can she stop Ricky Torres from teasing her? He calls her "four-eyes" and "bat-woman." Ricky soon learns that it isn't nice to tease someone just because she has to wear glasses.

Stewart, Molly Mia. *The Twins' Big Pow-Wow.* Bantam Skylark, 1993. (Sweet Valley Kids #44)

Elizabeth and Jessica are identical twins on the outside, but not on the inside, in their likes and dislikes. Elizabeth loves animals, woods, and muddy soccer games. Jessica likes stuffed animals, tea parties, and pretty clothes. They are spending Thanksgiving weekend on a Mojave reservation, where they meet Gray Eagle and his granddaughter, Ann. Ann lives on the reservation but doesn't want anything to do with the Indian culture. Elizabeth and Jessica help Ann learn to appreciate her roots.

BIBLIOGRAPHY

This list is intended to show the diversity and the multitude of series titles. It is not intended to be a complete list. The numbers of books is based on information available as of the fall of 1995.

Amelia Bedelia (Peggy Parish): 10 titles

American Girls Collection
    Christmas Stories: 5 titles
    Family Stories: 5 titles
    School Stories: 5 titles
    Spring Stories: 5 titles
    Summer Stories: 5 titles
    Winter Stories: 5 titles
    Pastimes (Cookbooks): 5 titles
    Pastimes (Craftbooks): 5 titles

Anastasia (Lois Lowry): 10 titles

Angel Park (Dean Hughes)
    All-Stars: 10 titles
    Hoop Stars: 4 titles
    Soccer Stars: 4 titles

Angelina (Katharine Holabird): 8 titles

Anne of Green Gables (L. M. Montgomery): 8 titles

Arthur Adventure (Marc Brown): 20 titles

Baby-Sitters Club (Ann M. Martin): 107 titles

Baby-Sitters Little Sister (Ann M. Martin): 56 titles

Baseball Legends: 40 titles

Black Stallion (Walter Farley): 10 titles

Bobbsey Twins (Laura Lee Hope): 8 titles

Boxcar Children Mysteries (Gertrude Chandler): 34 titles

Cam Jansen (David A. Adler): 14 titles

Choose Your Own Adventures: 53 titles

Chronicles of Narnia (C. S. Lewis): 7 titles

Downtown America: 24 titles

Draw 50 Books (Lee J. Ames): 16 titles

Encyclopedia Brown (Donald J. Sobol): 18 titles

Encyclopedia of Presidents: 41 titles

Eyewitness Books: 66 titles

Eyewitness Explorers: 12 titles

Eyewitness Juniors: 25 titles

Eyewitness Visual Dictionaries: 18 titles

Football Legends: 12 titles

Ghost Writer: 7 titles

Goosebumps (R. L. Stine): 45 titles

Great Brain (John D. Fitzgerald): 7 titles

Great Illustrated Classics: 40 titles

Hardy Boys Mystery Stories (Franklin Dixon): 58 titles

Henry and Mudge (Cynthia Rylant): 14 titles

Kids of the Polk Street School (Patricia Reilly Giff): 16 titles

Know Your Government: 43 titles

Littles (John Peterson): 11 titles

Lyle (Bernard Waber): 7 titles

Madeline (Ludwig Bemelmans): 7 titles

Maple Street Five: 8 titles

Meet the Author: 12 titles

Nancy Drew Mystery Stories (Carolyn Keene): 41 titles

Nate the Great (Marjorie Weinman Sharmat): 14 titles

Paddington Bear (Michael Bond): 10 titles

Pee Wee Scouts (Judy Delton): 20 titles

Pinky and Rex (James Howe): 7 titles

The Polka Dot Private Eye (Patricia Reilly Giff): 8 titles

Ramona Quimby (Beverly Cleary): 7 titles

Rookie Biographies (Carol Greene): 46 titles

Rotten Ralph (Jack Gantos): 7 titles

Saddle Club (Bonnie Bryant): 12 titles

Sebastian Super Sleuth (Mary Blount): 10 titles

Soup (Robert Newton Peck): 8 titles

Stepping Stone Books: 18 titles

Sweet Valley High (Kate William): 117 titles

Sweet Valley Kids (Molly Mia Stewart): 47 titles

Sweet Valley Twins (Jamie Suzanne): 48 titles

Sweet Valley Twins and Friends (Jamie Suzanne): 35 titles

Winnie-the-Pooh (A. A. Milne): 17 titles

Young Indiana Jones Chronicles: 13 titles

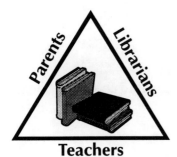

Chapter 14

Conclusion

ODDS AND ENDS

How about varying the meeting format? Ask local experts—public librarian, story-teller, local bookstore owner, or educator—to make presentations. Invite children to attend a session with their parents to discuss the current topic. Invite a local author, illustrator, or poet to attend. Vary the meeting time, have a "bring-a-friend" meeting—whatever will boost attendance and keep members active.

Can you add materials and canvass your members? Once the club has started, be aware of possible articles of interest in magazines and newspapers. Ask your club members to watch also. Add articles to those suggested in this book so that you keep current and aware of publishing trends. Survey parents and club members, both formally and informally, and see what their interests and concerns are. The topics included in this book are a direct response to the needs and concerns of the members of our own book club.

ADDITIONAL TOPICS

The following is a list of some other possible topics for meetings. Find topics of special interest to you and your community.

Book reports
Careers
Comic books
Folklore
Humor
Individual author
Mythology
Physically and emotionally challenged
    characters and persons
Sports stories
Summer reading

Travel
Values
    Controversial topics
    Gender bias
    Moral choices
    Portrayal of parents/adults
    Social issues
Your state
    authors residing in your state
    stories set in your state

QUESTIONNAIRE

1. Did you find the meetings useful? Do you feel more knowledgeable about the books available for your child?

_____

_____

2. Were you satisfied with the format of the meetings? _____

_____

3. Which topic was most interesting? (Horror, Historical Fiction, Multicultural, Science Fiction, Biography, Award Books)

_____

4. Were the handouts helpful? _____

_____

5. How can we generate more interest within our school community?

_____

_____

6. Were you satisfied with the frequency of the meetings? _____

_____

7. Would you be willing to join us next year? _____

8. Please list any topics you would like to see discussed in future meetings. (Summer Reading, Book Reports, How Parents Are Portrayed in Children's Fiction, Picture Books for Younger Children, Stereotyping, Boys vs. Girls, etc.)

_____

_____

_____

9. General Comments: _____

_____

_____

_____

Thank you!

From *The Reading Connection.* © 1997. Libraries Unlimited. (800) 237-6124.

REFERENCE LIST FOR TEACHERS AND PARENTS

Albyn, Carole Lisa, and Lois Sinaiko Webb. *The Multicultural Cookbook for Students*. Oryx Press, 1993.

Barstow, Barbara, and Judith Riggle. *Beyond Picture Books: A Guide to First Readers*. R. R. Bowker, 1995.

Bauer, Caroline Feller. *Celebrations: Read-Aloud Holiday and Theme Book Programs*. H. W. Wilson, 1985.

Benedict, Susan, and Lenore Carlisle. *Beyond Words: Picture Books for Older Readers and Writers*. Heinemann, 1992.

Berman, Matt. *What Else Should I Read? Guiding Kids to Good Books, Volume 1*. Libraries Unlimited, 1995.

Bernhardt, Edythe. *ABC's of Thinking with Caldecott Books*. Book Lures, 1988.

Blass, Rosanne, and Nancy E. Allen Jurenka. *Responding to Literature, Activities for Grades 6, 7, 8*. Teacher Ideas Press, 1991.

Bodart, Joni. *Booktalk! Booktalking and School Visiting for Young Adult Audiences*. H. W. Wilson, 1980.

Borba, Michele, and Dan Ungaro. *Bookends: Activities, Centers, Contracts, and Ideas Galore to Enhance Children's Literature*. Good Apple, 1982.

Buhler, Cheryl, Nolan Fossum, and Paula Spence. *An Annotated Bibliography of Thematic Literature*. Teacher Created Materials, 1993.

Carroll, Joyce Armstrong. *Poetry Book: Reading, Writing, Listening, Speaking, Viewing, and Thinking*. Teacher Ideas Press, 1995.

Cummings, Renee. *Multicultural Literature-Based Reading*. Instructional Fair, Inc., 1993.

Devers, William, and James Cipielewski. *Every Teacher's Thematic Booklist*. Scholastic Professional, 1993.

Donavin, Denise Perry, ed. *American Library Association: Best of the Best for Children*. Random House, 1992.

Dreyer, Sharon Spredemann. *The Bookfinder: When Kids Need Books*. American Guidance Service, 1985.

Fredericks, Anthony D. *Involving Parents Through Children's Literature: Grades 5-6*. Teacher Ideas Press, 1993.

Freeman, Judy. *Books Kids Will Sit Still For: A Guide to Using Children's Literature for Librarians, Teachers, and Parents*. Alleyside Press, 1984.

Gillespie, John T., and Corrine J. Naden. *Best Books for Children Preschool Through Grade 6*. R. R. Bowker, 1994.

———. *Juniorplots Four: A Book Talk Guide for Use with Readers Ages 12-16*. R. R. Bowker, 1992.

Huck, Charlotte S., Susan Hepler, and Janet Hickman. *Children's Literature in the Elementary School*. Harcourt Brace College, 1993.

Kollar, Judith L. *An Annotated Bibliography of Multicultural Literature*. Teacher Created Materials, 1993.

Lima, Carolyn W., and John A Lima. *A to Zoo: Subject Access to Children's Picture Books.* R. R. Bowker, 1993.

Lipson, Eden Ross. *The New York Times Parent's Guide to the Best Books for Children.* Times Books, 1988.

MacDonald, Margaret Read. *Booksharing: 101 Programs to Use with Preschoolers.* Library Professional Publications, 1988.

McArthur, Janice, and Barbara McGuire. *Using Literature Genres, Grades 4-6.* Frank Schaffer, 1995.

McElmeel, Sharron L. *An Author a Month (For Pennies).* Libraries Unlimited, 1988.

——. *Bookpeople: A First Album.* Teacher Ideas Press, 1990.

——. *Great New Nonfiction Reads.* Libraries Unlimited, 1995.

——. *The Latest and Greatest Read-Alouds.* Libraries Unlimited, 1994.

——. *McElmeel Booknotes: Literature Across the Curriculum.* Teacher Ideas Press, 1993.

Miller-Lachmann, Lyn. *Our Family, Our Friends, Our World: An Annotated Guide to Significant Multicultural Books for Children and Teenagers.* R. R. Bowker, 1992.

Paulin, Mary Ann. *Creative Uses of Children's Literature.* Library Professional Publications, 1982.

Polette, Nancy. *Teaching Critical Reading with Children's Literature.* Book Lures, 1988.

Polkingharn, Anne T., and Catherine Toohey. *More Creative Encounters: Activities to Expand Children's Responses to Literature.* Libraries Unlimited, 1988.

Price, Anne, and Juliette Yaakov. *Middle and Junior High School Library Catalog.* H. W. Wilson, 1995.

Raines, Shirley C., and Robert J. Candy. *More Story S-T-R-E-T-C-H-E-R-S: More Activities to Expand Children's Favorite Books.* Gryphon House, 1991.

Reuter, Janet. *Creative Teaching Through Picture Books for Middle School Students.* Frank Schaffer, 1993.

Rochman, Hazel. *Against Borders.* American Library Association, 1993.

Ryan, Connie. *Hooked on Books: A Genre-Based Guide for 30 Adolescent Books.* Frank Schaffer, 1993.

Schurr, Sandra, and Imogene Forte. *Using Favorite Picture Books to Stimulate Discussion and Encourage Critical Thinking.* Incentive, 1995.

Sitarz, Paula Gaj. *Picture Book Story Hours from Birthdays to Bears.* Libraries Unlimited, 1987.

——. *More Picture Book Story Hours from Parties to Pets.* Libraries Unlimited, 1990.

Spirt, Diana L. *Introducing Bookplots 3: A Book Talk Guide for Use with Readers Ages 8-12.* R. R. Bowker, 1988.

Stangl, Jean. *Story Sparklers (Starters and Extenders for 66 Noted Children's Picture Books).* T. S. Denison, 1991.

Trelease, Jim. *Hey! Listen to This: Stories to Read-Aloud.* Viking, 1992.

——. *The New Read-Aloud Handbook: Including a Giant Treasury of Great Read-Aloud Books.* Penguin Books, 1989.

——. *Read All About It! Great Read-Aloud Stories, Poems, and Newspaper Pieces for Preteens and Teens.* Penguin Books, 1993.

Vick, Diane. *Favorite Authors of Young Adult Fiction.* Frank Schaffer, 1995.

Wendelin, Karla Hawkins, and M. Jean Greenlaw. *Storybook Classrooms: Using Children's Literature in the Learning Center.* Humanics, 1986.

Woolman, Bertha, and Patricia Litsey. *The Newbery Award Winners: The Books and Their Authors.* T. S. Denison, 1992.

Yaakov, Julliette, ed. *Children's Catalog.* H. W. Wilson, 1991.

HELPFUL INTERNET ADDRESSES

This is a list of possible sites to visit or subscribe to. It is not meant to be a comprehensive list.

CHILDREN'S LITERATURE WEB GUIDE
    World Wide Web: http://www.ucalgary.ca/~dkbrown?index.html

THE INTERNET PUBLIC LIBRARY
    World Wide Web: http://ipl.sils.umich.edu/

J.R.R. TOLKIEN INFORMATION PAGE
    World Wide Web: www.ucalgary.ca/u/relipper/tolkien/rootpage.html

KIDLINK GOPHER
    Telnet: kids.ccit.duq.edu

KIDPUB (publications by children)
    World Wide Web: http://www.en-garde.com/kidpub

KIDSCOM
    World Wide Web: http://www.spectracom.com/kidscom

MYTHS AND LEGENDS
    World Wide Web: http://theocean.uoregon.edu/~myth

ONLINE CHILDREN'S BOOKS
    World Wide Web: http://www.digimark.net/iatech

PROJECT GUTENBERG
    World Wide Web: http://med.amsa.bu.edu/Gutenbert/Welcome.html

THE R.L. STINE HOME PAGE
    World Wide Web: http://scholastic.com:2005/public/Stine Home.html

THE SCHOLASTIC NETWORK
    World Wide Web: http://scholastic.com:2005/public/Home Page.html

TALES OF WONDER
    World Wide Web: http://www.ece.ucdavis.edu/~darsie/tales.html

TEACHER TALK
World Wide Web: http://www.mightymedia.com

UNCLE BOB'S KIDS PAGE
World Wide Web: http://gagme.wwa.com/~boba/kids.html

WORLD WIDE WEB VIRTUAL LITERATURE LIBRARY
World Wide Web: http://sunsite.unc.edu/ibic/TBIC-omepage,html

WRITINGS BY YOUNG PEOPLE
World Wide Web: http://www.calgary.ca/~dkbrown/writings.html

Mailing Lists

CHILDREN'S BOOK DISCUSSIONS
br_cafe@micronet.wcu.edu

CHILDREN'S LITERATURE: CRITICISM AND THEORY
childlit@rutvml.rutgers.edu

EDUCATIONAL RESOURCES ON THE INTERNET
c-edres@unbvml.csd.unb.ca

KIDSPHERE
kidsphere@vms.cis.pitt.edu

LIBRARY MEDIA SPECIALISTS
lm_net@suvm.syr.edu

LITERATURE FOR CHILDREN AND YOUTH
kidlit-l@bingvmb.cc.binghamton.edu

STUDENT BOOK REVIEWS (K-12)
Br_review@micronet.wcu.edu